# THE UNCLOUDED MIND

*Spiritual Insights For Personal
Development and Healing*

*Dear Elise,
Thank You For
your Support
Love Laura*

LAURA MCGEE-CHIUSANO

BALBOA
PRESS

A DIVISION OF HAY HOUSE

Copyright © 2015 Laura McGee-Chiusano.

All rights reserved. No part of this book may be used or reproduced by any means, graphic, electronic, or mechanical, including photocopying, recording, taping or by any information storage retrieval system without the written permission of the author except in the case of brief quotations embodied in critical articles and reviews.

Balboa Press books may be ordered through booksellers or by contacting:

Balboa Press
A Division of Hay House
1663 Liberty Drive
Bloomington, IN 47403
www.balboapress.com
1 (877) 407-4847

Because of the dynamic nature of the Internet, any web addresses or links contained in this book may have changed since publication and may no longer be valid. The views expressed in this work are solely those of the author and do not necessarily reflect the views of the publisher, and the publisher hereby disclaims any responsibility for them.

The author of this book does not dispense medical advice or prescribe the use of any technique as a form of treatment for physical, emotional, or medical problems without the advice of a physician, either directly or indirectly. The intent of the author is only to offer information of a general nature to help you in your quest for emotional and spiritual well-being. In the event you use any of the information in this book for yourself, which is your constitutional right, the author and the publisher assume no responsibility for your actions.

Any people depicted in stock imagery provided by Thinkstock are models, and such images are being used for illustrative purposes only. Certain stock imagery © Thinkstock.

Print information available on the last page.

ISBN: 978-1-5043-4578-1 (sc)
ISBN: 978-1-5043-4580-4 (hc)
ISBN: 978-1-5043-4579-8 (e)

Library of Congress Control Number: 2015919037

Balboa Press rev. date: 11/20/2015

# Foreword

> Here we see another bird escaped from the hunter's net.
> Once the Buddha said,
> "Blind is this world;
> Few see clearly here.
> As birds who escape from the net are few,
> Few go to heaven."
> —*The Dhammapada*, 174

All religions are not the same. Buddhism is not a religion in the sense of theistic religions, which were considered "the opiate of the masses" by Karl Marx. Nor is it a mystic teaching to promote mysticism or a ritualistic teaching to promote rituals. (Though without knowing the real teachings of the Buddha, some followers are engaged in various rituals.) For those who prefer to use the term *religion* for Buddhism, it is a humanistic or a realistic religion that teaches us how to know and see reality as it is.

Because people do not understand the essence of Buddhism—the real teachings of the Buddha—they mystify it. The Buddha demystified all mystic teachings and cleared the path through three fundamental principles: the Four Noble Truths, Dependent Origination, and the Three Characteristics of Existence.

He taught us a path to happiness. That is the Noble Eightfold Path, also known as the Middle Path. This is the path to be followed by all who wish for a peaceful, successful, and prosperous secular life and spiritual life.

Among all beings who walk on the earth, humans possess minds that can be developed further through proper exercises and meditation. In order to develop the mind, one has to understand the significance of spirituality. In this fast-moving, technically and materially advanced society, even the word *spirituality* is quite unfriendly to many.

Nevertheless, there is a silver lining in the dark cloud. There are those in our new generation, especially the truth seekers, who seek spirituality, the real Dhamma, and strive to understand what is Dhamma and what is not Dhamma. As the Buddha once said, "He who sees the Dhamma sees the Buddha." Those who see the true Dhamma are few, like the birds that escape from the net of the hunter.

We see an escaped bird, as mentioned in the poem above, in Laura McGee Chiusano, a social worker and a therapist. Her new gift to us is this book, *The Unclouded Mind*. She has written it as a spiritual seeker's insights on consciousness because she herself is conscientious in leading a spiritual life and therefore leads a life with a pacified mind.

In this book, Laura suggests to us the significance of leading a spiritual life and explores the meaning of the afterlife. With her knowledge acquired through many a book read on different religions and spiritual leaders, the significance of spirituality and oneness of mankind is clear to her. Every religion and every spiritual master teaches us spirituality. In this book, she has ably put together the relevant pieces of the puzzle of spiritual life.

For the accomplishment of this effort, the writer has selected eight different topics:

1. Awakening
2. Perception
3. The ego
4. Mindfulness
5. Manifesting the good
6. Time
7. Beyond the body
8. Soul to soul

The writer says, "The stirrings of a new level of consciousness have begun for many individuals; this is commonly referred to as *awakening*. Awakening is the inner signal telling us that it is time to delve deeper into the mystery of life and start remembering who we really are and why we are here. An awakening also unveils the ability to manifest and tap into the true gifts with which we come into this lifetime. First and foremost, it rekindles our knowing and conscious contact with the God within us. These new insights are our birthrights from the divine creative source. ... Don't ignore those feelings that cause you to respond with incredulity or doubt. Pay attention to them. Don't be afraid to change things up a bit; move one single step closer to a source that will fuel further investigation and deeper seeking. The source could be a class, a book, an article, or a film."

According to the teaching of the Buddha, you are your own master. With the right understanding of her inner feelings, the writer tells us, "All of the high glory of God and creation is still within you; your soul knows that well. ... Sometimes going back to our roots helps us slow down the craziness of life. Sometimes going back even further helps us understand why the craziness developed in the first place. I have found it helpful to develop a philosophy by which I try to live my life, a set of guiding principles. No one has forced them upon me or suggested that if I don't follow them, I will suffer some consequences. They are my standards for me. I follow the basic standards of Buddhism called the Eightfold Path and the Five Precepts."

The writer makes clear that "perception is the main determiner of how your day will go, how your year will go, and how your entire life will go."

The writer talks about mindfulness in daily life. *Mindfulness* is the watchword, the key in the teachings of the Buddha. Accordingly, the Buddha has taught four establishments of mindfulness, which bring us solace and peace throughout life, and final liberation.

Time is another very significant and relevant topic dealt with here. Everything exists within time and space. Through vipassanā meditation, Buddhism teaches us the way to go beyond time and space.

Finally, the writer presents a new subject, which is re-becoming (rebirth). We become again and again in new lives because there are many different life systems in the universe. According to Buddhist cosmology, there are thirty-one different existences in the universe. In these realms, we become different beings again and again because of craving and attachment. If one would completely cut off craving and attachment, one would have no more re-becoming. With the realization of this, one can declare, "Birth is destroyed, the spiritual life has been lived, done what had to be done; there will be no coming to this world hereafter."

Read this book with an open mind; it will help you lead a spiritual life, be happy, and be peaceful in the present moment. Living in the present moment is the teaching of the Buddha. The present moment is the most precious moment. We wish blessings upon Laura for the success of her life and finally the realization of supreme bliss.

May all beings be well, happy, and peaceful!

Bhikkhu T. Seelananda
Bhavana Society Forest Monastery
97 Meditation Trail
High View, WV 26808
seela22bhavana@gmail.com

# IMPERMANENCE

In every form I see in the billowing white clouds,
I see the wonder and also the impermanence.
Every thought is as fleeting as the shape-shifting clouds.
The glorious moments of love, joy, and passion are as temporary
as the moments of anger, pain, and unpleasantness.
It's a choice to cling to either.
For some, the tendency to cling tightly
to the pain,
is as critical as clinging to
the wonderful happy moments
Freedom from both of them is what lightens our paths.
Freedom of the burden of those moments,
We can find the bliss in just this one moment.

# Preface

> I asked why I have received only this.
> A voice replied, only this will lead to that.
> —Rumi

As I weighed the decision to move forward with publishing this book, I had to ask myself a big question. Given the amount of self-help, spiritual, and new-age books available for people to read, I asked, "What's so special about me that might make me a source of spiritual insights or lessons?" The answer is not a thing and everything.

As far as religion goes, I circumvented all traditional methods of spiritual education and learning. I believed spirituality was religion, and I had no affiliation with either. I grew up relatively poor in a town on Long Island called Selden. Saying you're from Selden gives people a little snapshot of where you come from and a response that is sometimes verbalized as "Oh, you're from Selden," with a tone of partly pity and partly degradation. When I was younger, I didn't know that Selden people were regarded so poorly. Not until I was much older did I figure it out and experience the perception of those not from Selden.

My mother was single after making the courageous decision to leave my alcoholic father when I was five years old. She worked as a waitress to keep a roof over our heads and give me as much as she could. We moved a lot, and I went to about ten schools over the course of my public school education. We were on what was then commonly referred to as "welfare." Back then, food stamps looked like Monopoly money. There were no debit cards then, so every time we bought something, it was obvious we were on welfare and probably poor.

When I was eighteen, I'd just graduated high school and was with my best friend, Eileen, when the unthinkable happened. It was August 9, 1979. I remember the day vividly as those who have experienced a traumatic event often do. I was driving with Eileen back to my house from hers after watching *General Hospital*, going home to feed and tend to my two beloved dogs, Duchess and Scruffy. It was the era of Luke and Laura; back when there were no DVD players or VCRs.

As we approached my house, a bratty little girl said, "Your house burned down, and your dogs are dead." It was true! My house was smoldering, and my precious dogs were gone. I was in such shock I nearly drove into a tree. The police were there, and they prevented me from going into the charred remains of our house.

There were no cell phones then, so I had to go into a neighbor's house that I didn't know to call my mother at work at the diner. I was hysterical as I told her our house burned down, my dogs were gone and we were homeless. We were renters and we had no rental insurance. It was all gone. It was really at that point, I was sure there was no God, and if there was one, I didn't want anything to do with him. He was no friend of mine. I had no hope, and as for God, I had a few choice words for him.

These events, and many others, of course, had a lasting impact on my life and my spiritual perspectives. I hadn't even realized how long they impacted me until I bought my home some twenty-two years after that experience. It was then the fear of losing my home again rose up to greet me as my poverty mentality suggested I had no business owning a home. After all, I was just a poor kid from Selden. It was in that moment, I knew I had to radically change that belief and distorted perception or I would certainly wind up creating a self-fulfilling prophecy for the worst. I'm happy to say that since then I've consciously manifested an abundant and happy life.

I've learned a lot (thankfully!) over the past twenty years that I hope to share with others to inspire them and help them believe in the unbelievable when they have little hope and even less faith. I've learned that everyone has a story about who they believe they are, what they have done, and the tragedies they've endured. Everyone believes for a while that they are those stories, and in some ways they are. As the great trance medium Edgar Cayce stated in so many of his readings, every action, thought, and deed is imprinted for eternity on the "skeins of time."

There comes a time, however, when you may need to change your affiliation with that story, especially if holding on to it creates suffering. A knowing deep in my soul made it clear that it was necessary for all the bad stuff to happen as it did to get me to the inspired place where I am in today. That is why I chose the Rumi quote for the epigraph of this preface; it so perfectly fits my life: "I asked, why I have received only this. A voice replied, only this will lead to that."

So back to the original question I posed: What makes me believe that I have anything to offer about spirituality, spiritual awakenings, consciousness, or God? Well, the answer is I suffered greatly: I endured pains and uncertainties, and I hated and judged others and myself harshly. Then I learned to forgive and just do the next right thing; I learned to believe in things you can't see and to have faith and stay present and conscious of every breath during the rough times. I've learned how to dream big and know that Spirit has bigger dreams for me than I can even imagine.

All I have to do is my part, step by little step, leap by leap, and the universe will do it's part on my behalf. Now I am thriving. I have overridden the fears and anxieties of being poor and all that goes with abandonment and rejection as a child. I'm still that kid from Selden, but I'm also so much more. I'll never forget the tougher times, but I access them for the greater good of others. As a psychotherapist, I spend every day trying to help others see that they too are more than those early beginnings of their lives. I encourage them to overcome obstacles by recognizing their own birthright of happiness, success and joy.

On the wall in my office, I have a revised version of an Emily Dickinson poem, "I Shall Not Live in Vain." I try to live by the sentiment expressed in it:

> If I can stop one heart from breaking
> I shall not live in vain
> Or ease one life the aching
> Or cool one pain
> Or help one lonely person
> Find happiness again,
> I shall not live in vain.

I'm able to embrace all the events in my life today and be thankful for all the experiences I've had, knowing that each one brought me to the amazing life I have now. I hope this little book can give you—no matter what your circumstances have been or what they are now—a moment of understanding of who you truly are on a much grander level than you had imagined.

Maybe this little book can keep one soul from aching, so my life is not in vain.

# Introduction

There was a time not so long ago, I didn't understand what spirituality was. I certainly didn't have any religious affiliation, and I abhorred the thought of any. I really didn't have a spiritual life that I knew of. But I have recently figured out that was untrue.

This is very old news for the many individuals who teach, practice, and write about spirituality. But for me, it was a timely if not long overdue epiphany. It was as though something in me woke up, and I have been *mostly* awake and *mostly* mindful ever since. We all have a spiritual life. Whether we choose to interact within it or to reject it really doesn't make a difference; we are all spiritual beings. So often in the hardest moments of life, most of us start looking for answers. This is exactly what happened to me. I was compelled, truly compelled, to move into seeking information. Initially I didn't know what or whom I was seeking. I can only describe myself as someone on a precipice, reaching out as far as an arm can reach into the infinite sky. My seeking included reading vast amounts of literature on all things having to do with the big questions: Why I am here? Who are these people popping into my life and creating conflicts and havoc? It almost seemed that the information I was reading was being downloaded into my mind. Each book I read led to another and another.

Then I started to try to understand my own questions: Why did certain circumstance and people show up when they did? Was it purposeful, or is life just one big coincidence? I went to mediums and psychics and had a past-life regression. People thought I'd lost my grip, spending a lot of money to find ... something. But what?

One night I was given a small bit of information to reawaken my then sleeping interest in spirituality. As a social worker in a drug treatment program, I was given many opportunities to awaken, but that night was the one that opened the door. Two people in one of my groups were talking about someone named Abraham. I had no idea what they were talking about, but it was clearly a show of support from one person to another to help with their recoveries. I asked, "Who is Abraham?" Then they asked me a series of questions. Had I ever heard of the law of attraction? Had I ever heard of Esther Hicks? I'd never heard of either.

One person in the group suggested I watched a film called *What the Bleep Do We Know?* and dig up a book called *The Law of Attraction*, by Esther and Jerry Hicks. (This was before the film *The Secret* came out.) Having believed I was running my own life, I'd never stumbled upon either. My reaction of "Hmmm …" was enough to get me to rent the movie and read the book. I took the bait, so to speak, and haven't let go of it since.

Ever the analyst, I can and have asked myself why that information on that night from that individual took hold in my psyche when, during for the previous twenty years of my adulthood, nothing had. The answer is timing, of course. Not clock time but divine timing. It was time for me to begin to awaken and to raise my vibration and spiritual consciousness.

As my spiritual studies went deeper, I could see clearly a crossroad where all the teachings come together. I read and learned more about Buddhist teachings. I have since become a student of Buddhism and a novice practitioner. One of my dear friends is a Buddhist monk from Sri Lanka. (It's no coincidence we share the same birth date.)

I also read books by authors who have been considered spiritual teachers, such as Edgar Cayce, Deepak Chopra, Wayne Dyer, Neville Goddard, William Walker Atkinson, Eckhart Tolle, Gary Zukav, Epictetus, Plato, Robert Louis Stevenson, Madame Helena Blavatsky, and Brian Weiss. They became what consumed me for months at a time. I read Neale Donald Walsch's trilogy, *Conversations with God*, in less than seventy-two hours … the trilogy! When I got my first Kindle, in one month I read thirty-two books by those authors and many others. I was hooked. I read copious amounts of books on reincarnation, astrology, past-life regressions, and any other metaphysical phenomena. I read books that were written through channels from those who have crossed over, such as the great book by Anthony Borgia, *Life in the World Unseen*. I read ancient philosophy as well as old books on mediums and psychic attunement.

Then, somewhere in the midst of this insanity (that's what it felt like sometimes), a man introduced himself to me as my twin soul. I'd never heard of such a thing and frankly thought it was a unique pickup line. As a result, I felt thrust further into pivotal change, and constant urging from my soul to know and see and understand all that I possibly could about the soul.

One of the books I came across for a second time was a teaching called *A Course in Miracles* (ACIM). My first encounter with it had been a few years earlier. I tried to understand it, but I just wasn't ready. It was difficult for me to read and understand. I'd started with the workbook section and lasted only seventy-six days. Then I gave the book back. I didn't look at it again for well over a year. When I did decide to pick it up again I knew I was ready for the course's powerful teaching. That's when I started to really read and attempt to understand it. But more importantly, I wanted to incorporate the teachings and lessons into my life.

It's certainly not an easy book to read, but its teachings have been a great blessing in helping me change my attitude and mind-set toward life. I have since read or listened to ACIM several times. I listen to the audio version regularly during my travels in my car. Advanced teachers of ACIM such as Marianne Williamson, have been studying and incorporating the teachings for decades. I am a novice, albeit enthusiastic, student of ACIM at this point, and I make every effort to incorporate its magnificent guidance into my life daily.

One of its many wonderful teachings is that the ego is the cause of all pain and suffering. Interestingly, discourses on Buddhist teachings and principles also discuss the problems of the ego. Incorporating other readings on the ego and suffering led me to read about karma.

Edgar Cayce stated often in his readings that "the mind is the builder." He spoke extensively about reincarnation and found in his life readings that certain life circumstances serve as pathways to balancing out past-life debts to either a person or self. I fully believe and happily embrace that we agree to reincarnate with certain experiences in the plan. I love to call this the Divine Contract. I believe that this Divine Contract is agreed upon by all souls who incarnate to the earth plane. It helps us stay connected to our soul groups and directs the course of what we hope to accomplish along the way until we return Home.

As we develop and grow, we of course get to make decisions based on our free will. The decisions we make either add to not-so-good karma—"what we sow, so shall we reap"—or preferably, a lift and elevation elevate our soul. Nothing is random. How we choose to react to any given situation is up to us.

I love all discussions on reincarnation and the soul, spiritual progression, and past-life regression. I love hearing about and reading about people, especially kids, remembering past lives. These propelled me into reading anything from any era on the topic and happily finding out it has been written about for centuries. Plato, Marcus Aurelius, Ralph Waldo Emerson, W. Stainton Moses, Rumi, Emily Dickinson, Edgar Cayce, Brian Weiss, and the list goes on and on—all awakened to the knowing of reincarnation and wrote about it for the rest of us to awaken to. Some receive it and some reject it; either way is okay. We each ultimately reach the appropriate place of awakening for ourselves.

My many questions ultimately melded into just one: What is the meaning of my life? It is paradoxically one very little but enormous question. Maybe for all of us it is ultimately the same. The following pages are written simply to share experiences with others who are also beginning to feel nudges toward similar discoveries. Enjoy your journey!

# Awakening

> Do not be afraid of your difficulties.
> Do not wish you could be in other circumstances than you are.
> For when you have made the best of an adversity,
> it becomes the stepping stone to a splendid opportunity.
> —Helena Petrovna Blavatsky

The stirrings of a new level of consciousness have begun for many individuals; this is commonly referred to as *awakening*. This awakening is the inner signal telling us that it is time to delve deeper into the mystery of life and remember who we really are and why we are here. An awakening also unveils the ability to manifest and tap into the true gifts with which we come into this lifetime. First and foremost, it rekindles our knowing and conscious contact with the God within us. These new insights are our birthrights from the divine creative Source.

No matter what your religious beliefs or cultural practices are, no matter what you call the creative impulse—God, Buddha, Shakti, Shiva, or Allah—we all have the same opportunity to go beyond the limits of those beliefs and of those cultural practices. The challenge is to direct our paths so that we gain more and more awareness about the true nature of our being, our true self, our oneness with all.

Each inquiry and inspiration from our souls brings us closer to figuring the whole thing out—*if we are ready to know*. With each new awareness, and as we continue to investigate and seek more information about the meaning of these stirrings from our souls, we may experience the excitement of discovering this new information. But it isn't new! It has been known throughout the millennia and taught by great sages, wisdom teachers, philosophers, and spiritualists all along. The origins were often wrongly interpreted or concealed until the age of man allowed it without fear of punishment.

*The Secret,* which I really enjoyed, just hits the tip of the spiritual iceberg. It introduces a new way of perceiving and directing the course of our lives. It encourages us to learn how to use our innate energies and vibrations to create better circumstances for ourselves. It focuses a lot on manifesting material things, such as a new car or home or attractive mate. It leaves a lot out regarding the power of our thoughts and feelings to create our entire lives. The secret of *The Secret* is that it isn't actually a secret. So the real secret remains, a secret, yet one that is fully available to all who seek it. Unless you really start to investigate and change some outmoded beliefs, you risk being an unknowing creating force, and the outcomes could go either way.

The spiritual search I've found myself on has brought me the realization that every dream I have is being created, and the more excited I get about it, the closer it is at hand. As you get warmer and closer to doctrines you once believed to be concealed, you also begin to feel an enthusiasm that will overflow. For me, that enthusiasm sometimes borders on giddiness. The secret is much bigger than the movie called *The Secret* could ever make palpable. It is more than mere words can even explain or verbalize; words are only symbols that, in reality, limit the limitless, the infinite, and the eternal. All the creative impulses of the heavens are within each and every one of us. All you have to do is feel it with every cell of your being and on every level of thought.

For me, the assurance that the conditions of my life have not been random, but instead were fully manifested by divine thought, has been very freeing. I know that as a result of a well-deliberated process, the trials I've faced are lessons I've needed in order to gain mastery over my challenges. I know distress is just an opportunity to choose again. Lifetime after lifetime, we are set upon a journey to make better choices and to reawaken from our slumber. Often, it's hard for people to look at things that they judge as *injustices* and see them instead as *opportunities* not only for their own individual soul's growth but ultimately for the collective soul's growth as well. Few people have embraced this view. I wish I'd remembered it years ago. It's so significant a spiritual concept that, in its fullest potential, it rattles the ego structure of the person who chooses to embraces it.

The wonderful Wayne Dyer, author of *The Power of Intention* and many other books about intention, manifesting, and creating a different life for yourself (including *Change your Thoughts, Change Your Life*), introduced me to another inspirational source of creativity: Neville Goddard. Neville (as he is identified in his books) explains the creative power within us as well as our oneness with the ultimate creating source, God. It isn't only about manifesting a new car, a million dollars, or an ideal mate; Neville teaches us that it's the *feeling* we are looking for.

We are first and foremost sensory beings. Because we feel (and we want to feel good feelings), we look to our feelings to assess our physical and emotional lives. We look for the feeling that an ideal mate can evoke in us, the feeling that a more spacious home would bring us, the feeling of being a part of a large, loving family, or the feeling of being famous. We create our feelings, and they either give rise to our betterment or propel our downward spiral. *We must take responsibility for both.* Our life experience is about figuring out that we can reach our fullest and limitless potential. In this holy instant of our lives, we can achieve so much more than we believe we can. We must have active imaginations, and to succeed, our imaginations must be backed by our enthusiasm about what we want to experience in our lives. It also helps to learn how to raise our energetic vibrations to what they will be once we achieve the desired outcome.

Basically, we need to feel it from the end—that is, feel it from the perspective of having achieved the goal, even if we haven't quite reached it yet. For me, this is the knowing that my every breath, thought, word, deed, feeling, and reaction is being overseen by a loving source and by my higher self from beyond my physical body. The recognition of my ability to have an expanded consciousness is one of the greatest and most freeing discoveries of my fifty-three years. This expanded consciousness helps me access my unlimited potential. To know that you can expand your consciousness to the fullest extent of the physical plane as well as some levels of the spiritual planes and then, endlessly and without limit, to do so on the celestial planes is the way to begin to live without fear and apprehension.

So if the stirrings to *awaken* have begun in you, allow them also to inspire *movement* within you. Movement leads to investigation, which can ultimately lead to conscious manifestations. Pay attention to your internal guide; often I find that people experience anxiety when their internal guidance system is being ignored or overridden. Don't ignore those feelings that cause you to respond with incredulity or doubt. Pay attention to them. Don't be afraid to change things up a bit; move one single step closer to a source that will fuel further investigation and deeper seeking. The source could be a class, a book, an article, or a film.

Don't allow your mind to be clouded by the past or other people's ideas, problems, expectations, and fears. Go out and find out what makes sense to *you*. If I feel I've drifted from the wonderful and divinely inspired knowledge that I've gained, I slow down for a tune-up. Usually, that tune-up starts with solitude and meditation. For me, silence is as necessary as the air I breathe. Often, reconnecting comes from rereading a book that has inspired me in the past or discovering an ancient teaching to validate that every part of life is necessary. I never want to drift away from believing in the sacredness of all life forms or the awareness of the connectedness we all share. Every book or teaching I've read, from ancient scribes to modern-day, new-age thinkers, validates this knowing.

None of us are wrong; we just find inspiration through different materials and messages and experiences. People draw inspiration from all manner of experiences. They find fulfillment through adventure (climbing Mount Everest) or compassion (working in a hospice or spending time with children or animals). *What inspires you?* If you can't answer this question almost instantly, maybe it's time for you to embark on your own investigation. Maybe your journey can start by reading this book. It can also be answered by experiencing some new things or re-experiencing things that once brought you joy and inspiration. Have you drifted away from what once drove you, due to the busyness of your life?

In many ways, the human experience is made up of two sides of ourselves: the inner life and outer life we all experience. Trying to figure out who we truly are and what we believe about any given situation is often difficult, especially if those two sides of self are not working in harmony.

The outer life consists of many things, some wonderful and some dismal. It is always the expression and physical manifestation of all our thoughts and perceptions. Even if we never verbalize them to another living soul, they still have the same potential to manifest. The outer life is the outward expression of all our mental dialogues and emotions—sometimes consciously, sometimes not so consciously.

The outer life uses the eyes to judge ourselves and the world we see and don't see. It is how we refer to ourselves or others, such as being a janitor, a teacher, a mailman. It is the names we have and the circumstances through which we move daily. It is the bounce in our step that we present to the world or the despair people see when they look into our eyes. The foods we enjoy and the music we dance to, our body type, our hair color, and even how we walk and talk all make up our outer life.

The inner life consists of our thoughts: our opinions, ideas, and judgments about our outer life and those in it. In it are our vast imaginative ability and our analytical mechanisms. Our inner life debates our judgments about our body type, our hair color, and how we walk and talk. It is our frustrations and fears that we dare not verbalize for fear that we will give them life. It is our secret desires and wishes. It is the unspoken inner voice that congratulates or condemns others and us. What are the conversations you have in your mind? What is the dialogue in that secret little space where no others know or have control over what you *really* think about them or yourself?

Which one are we: our outer life or our inner life? We are both our inner dialogue and the expression of it. As Neville Goddard stated, "Speech is the image of the mind." Both have enormous impact, but one is from the other, so the thought is the maker of it all. We're so much more than the expressions and contradictions of our inner life and our outer life. We are souls on a journey to reconnect with the divine while also learning how to negotiate all the levels of the physical forms that we may encounter.

We are our accumulated karma from the thousands of years we have journeyed into this physical life. We are the essence of each of those previous personalities of the soul. This essence, sometimes as gentle as a whisper or as strong as a tornado, is the cause and effect of previous lives. The Buddhist term for these intentional actions and their respective results is known as kamma or karma. As the Venerable Bhante Gunaratana wrote in his book *Eight Mindful Steps to Happiness,* "Even if you aren't worried about a future lifetime and just want to get what you can out of this one, it is still beneficial to do wholesome things and think wholesome and compassionate thoughts." This is the optimal blending of our inner life with our outer life.

As are the actions of a single-cell microorganism in response to its environments, so is all of life. As you know the goodness of one, you must know, too, that every single person has the same potential for goodness as every other person. As you recognize an evil in a person, know that every person has the same potential for evil—dormant perhaps, but lying in wait in the shadows. Your light is that same light you see in other people's eyes, but your darkness is also the darkness you see in them.

Awakening will certainly bring mindfulness to all your interactions. What any one life form manifests, so do all the others; the only difference is conscious choice and awareness. Within every seed is the intrinsic urge to reach its highest potential. The bud of a rose evolves to be the most fragrant and beautiful rose it can be. There is no trepidation in the life process that says, "There are so many other red roses on this bush; there isn't really a need for me." It blooms and it is a continual impetus for poetry and also for pain—as the thorn reminds us.

All life forms have active and inactive life cycles. We are the only ones that want to rush through or control every little cycle that we meet up with. Plants and animals have dormant seasons or periods of hibernation. Springtime is often the season that renews the life cycles of birth to decay. Humans also have dormant seasons where there is little evidence of growth until there are impulses for the renewal of life. The process of birth to decay follows, and the cycle begins again.

Nothing is random in this physical life. There is a rhythm and purpose to all things. There are no coincidences in this magnificent tapestry of life. It begins with a thought to be, and then the process of our incarnation begins.

The journey into life starts from the ascension. It is there our soul begins the process from the timeless ethereal to the time-bound physical. There are many levels of energy fields—from the high celestial bodies to the denser and closer-to-physical astral bodies, then ultimately the physical incarnation. And then the journey back to the original place of ascension or to the godhead starts again. This return to ascension begins with the now time-bound experiences of a lifetime and with each new lifetime. As we grow and learn in the physical, we do so in the astral and higher celestial levels as well.

Spiritual growth and development happen on all the levels. It's like going up a ladder when you are in the process of awakening and then down the ladder for rebirth and then up again. Each rung on the ladder that you leave off at is where your soul seeks to return—or to the higher rung, but definitely not lower.

So, if for some reason your journey into the physical takes an unpleasant turn downward, it also takes the same unpleasant turned downward on the other side. Not that you can't redeem yourself; of course you can. All of the high glory of God and creation is still within you; your soul knows that well. You've been given a glimmer of such glorious and blissful states that making a decision that lands you further from where you started is disheartening. It causes you to feel such a level of despondency spiritually that it's hard to feel worthy of the blessing from higher souls reaching out to you to get you on the next rung higher. This judgment is from your true self. It is not the judgment of any other being, such as guides or God or even family members who have gone before you.

As we come from the spirit realm into physical form, we must descend our spiritual levels prior to birth to be better prepared for the density of form and matter. We are taken down to the physical level by our master guide and others who stay with us throughout our journey in our body. The ascension or awakening process in our physical life is charted by reaching certain spiritual levels of development, much like the developmental stages that the psychologist Erik Erikson detailed in his theory of the eight stages of development. It is important that we master one stage before we can ascend to the next.

Once we move through the various spiritual lessons of our life, we hopefully begin the awakening. The path is more conscious. This is the beginning of remembering our true selves on a spiritual level and our desire for reconnection with the spiritual planes of existence. The afterlife ascension is the same as the life ascension from the point of awakening to the physical death of the body. Once we return home, we do so still desiring to be closer to the highest realms, the source of creation, or the highest divine spiritual light, God, or the universal Source. However we choose to identify the energy of creation, we yearn to reach that level once we leave the body.

Just as the time to awaken in this physical life is set, the time to release begins as the soul urges us to realize we are nearing our return home. I'm fascinated by the connectedness of the here and now and the hereafter through the union of souls in life and by the paths undertaken to reach our original or higher spiritual level. The very fabric of our physical selves is woven into the great tapestry of the universe. Everything that lives and breathes is woven together as one. There is no them and no me; there is no more mine; there is just a beautifully blended *we* that merges together. Nonduality is the oneness of our true essence in that there is no separation of anything or anyone. We are each here to offer a hand to someone who is struggling to get up the next rung spiritually, while also allowing ourselves to accept a hand from the soul on the rung above us.

The moment we return to our true home, we know if we completed our life mission and are received with "Well done. You lived your life well, used your time well, handled opportunities mindfully" or "Hmmm, I was surprised you made such a decision" or "We had hoped you felt our urgings for a different decision. What have you learned?" Some of it is difficult, and some of it is easy. We have enormous love, and we have deep sadness. With great love, sadness awaits. With deep sadness comes the opening of potential. With potential comes great opportunity. From opportunity we make a decision; once then we decide, we have made a choice. With each choice comes a consequence. With each consequence comes renewed understanding, and finally with renewed understanding *we reach compassion.*

We are all here to learn that particular lesson. Compassion is the soul's truth and greatest desire. We aren't designed for isolation. We're social beings who need other beings to help us grow and evolve and love.

Patience is required now as your continued growth is ensured. Some things can't be rushed. Like a car in a traffic jam, we must accept all conditions that arise and in that stillness know that we are still on our way home and that we will get home. Know that all is well on your journey, despite the brief or lengthy traffic jams of life.

Imagine, if you will, a great and variable pendulum. It swings far, far to the east and far, far to the west. In between the east and the west are any number of scenarios, circumstances, and choices. The swings of the pendulum of life tend to bring in, at the furthest reaches, chaos, indecision, and uncertainty. Call this time the adolescence of life—not necessarily based on a chronological age, but more on the experience of man. As with any time of adolescence, there are many experiences that can swing this pendulum drastically. Even the most minor event can cause it to swing to the extremes.

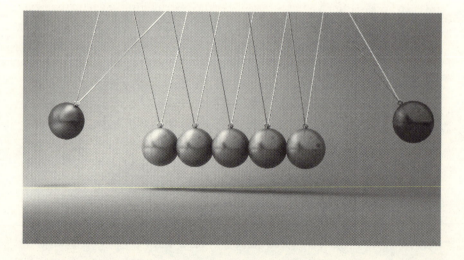

There are very few moments of stillness during this stage of man. During these times throughout history, there have been incredible fluxes in earthly stability. Individuals and countries exist in a constant state of uncertainty and reactivity—often even violent reactivity. Impulsivity is commonplace.

As in human adolescence, there are only occasional little sparks of insight and fleeting awarenesses. It's predominately a time when the ego is very reactive. This adolescence of man is represented by the desire for only the basic survival mechanisms of the ego in early life stages. Many lifetimes are needed to slow the swing of the pendulum during the adolescence of man. The gift of these drastic swings is the many opportunities presented for learning.

Then, with the advancement of the mind and attunements made very subtly with the Spirit or higher consciousness, the pendulum no longer swings from one extreme to the opposite extreme. It now has a slightly narrower berth. There are moments of awareness that not everything is random and unpredictable. This period may last a lifetime or even many lifetimes. This is called the maturing of man. He has now moved further along and upward in his level of consciousness and of knowing, moving from the stage of adolescence to maturity.

With this development, we are able to quiet our mind a little more and therefore control our reactions to the unpredictability of the pendulum. The opportunities of this period are focused growth and mindful intuition. There may still be times of fear and reactivity, but there will also be times of great joy and well-deliberated and earned happiness. With the slowing of the pendulum comes an awareness that you don't have to react impulsively or at all. There is a hint of having a unique purpose in life.

Then, finally, as the individual evolves to a higher level of awareness and his attunement with Spirit is all-knowing and flowing, and his mind is fully attuned to the higher vibrational impulses, the pendulum swings only very slightly east and very slightly west, but quickly returns to a still and quiet center. There are rarely any events on the material plane that can cause a return to the extreme swings of the adolescence of man or the still somewhat variable swings of the matured man. This stage of the experience represented by the pendulum of life is the experience of the inspired consciousness of man.

This stage involves knowing that you have a choice about how far the pendulum swings yet also that you are not in control of the pendulum of life swinging, and that is okay. There is a fearlessness that comes from the connection to Source, and an acceptance that even the most unpleasant experiences are divinely guided and purposeful. At this stage, we have faith that our path is certain. We also have a deep understanding and acceptance of our karmic path and our karmic relationships.

What can you do to still the pendulum in such a chaotic world? Well, first recognize the patterns of your life and see which are benefiting you and which aren't. From there you can begin to make changes. You have to be able to consider that there may be a better way in order to start looking for that way. Taking charge of the mind is not always an easy thing to do. In fact it can be quite challenging. People so often avoid silence or meditation or even alone time because they fear their own thoughts.

Many of my clients have been diagnosed with anxiety disorders and depression. They have been prescribed various medications basically to quiet their minds. There are certainly those who benefit tremendously from medication and thankfully there are wonderful doctors who understand the chemistry of the brain and the pharmaceuticals and are skilled at finding just the right medication for the best symptom management. Most people I work with are aware of meditation but won't attempt to experience it or practice it. The common concern is "I won't be able to not think of anything." Controlling the swings of the pendulum is not about "not thinking of anything" or walking through life as though covered in pixie dust and daisies. It's about developing an awareness that our thoughts and our perceptions are either working for us or working against us, for our betterment or for our undoing. At this stage of my life, I have very little tolerance for allowing my mind to run amuck. I must have those precious periods of stillness and quietness to allow the pendulum of my mind to be still.

It seems that human society has lost its spiritual interest and wisdom over thousands of years. This has distanced us from what ancient wisdom expressed through philosophers such as Plato, Socrates, and Aristotle as well as the ancient Stoics, such as Diogenes of Babylon and Marcus Aurelius. These familiar ancient philosophers wrote and taught extensively on the true nature of man and suggested how man best lives his life. They taught that the soul is the governing body of our life, not the mind. What ancient civilizations such as the Mayans and even the early Egyptians taught and believed about the spiritual meanings of life has often been regarded as mythical and useless in today's world. Every era and culture has had within it esoteric teachings that brought spiritual connection to their tribes and communities, and within their great halls.

More contemporary writers, such as William Walker Atkinson, wrote about the great Arcane school of thought. With his many pen names, he wrote prolifically on spiritual teachings, such as personal magnetism, the subconscious planes of the mind, and yogi philosophy. He talked extensively about the levels of consciousness that we can achieve.

Now, in our ultramodernized society, there's a tendency to focus on materialism and obtaining more of everything. Due to the rapid advances of technology, seemingly peaking to new heights at this time, individuals want instant gratification and instant results. We've become consumed with getting and getting fast. The focus on material gain and building an exaggerated self-image has brought about a much less tolerant and much more judgmental society.

Now the challenge is to find realistic ways to reverse those human flaws of judgment and intolerance into radical acceptance, nonjudgment, and tolerance of others. Sometimes going back to our roots helps us slow down the craziness of life. Sometimes going back even further helps us understand why the craziness developed in the first place. I've found it helpful to develop a philosophy by which I try to live, a set of guiding principles. No one has forced them upon me or suggested that if I don't follow them, I will suffer some consequences. They are my standards for me.

I follow the basic standards of Buddhism called the Eightfold Path and the Five Precepts. These offer a way to live a life of integrity, which is very important to me—both my own and the integrity of those I choose to associate with or invite into my life. I also remind myself (courtesy of Byron Katie in her insightful and inspiring book *The Work*) to mind my business and identify what is my business and what is someone else's and what is God's or the universe's. It simplifies life so much when you just mind your own business. This isn't the derogatory statement; it refers to being mindful of what really is your own business.

What is your philosophy for your life? Does it bring you happiness, love, and joy, or is it keeping those things from you? Take a few moments to consider the philosophy by which you live. Do you need to change it, or are you content with what it brings into your life? Assessing the current conditions of your life can help you determine the philosophy you are living by and if it has been beneficial for you or harmful.

# Perception

*People are not disturbed by things, but by the view they take of things.*

           Epictetus (AD 55–135)

What is perception? Perception is how we judge the world around us and its impact on the self. It is the vision and interpretation we create about people, places, and things we encounter along our life's journey. Changing our perspective, changes our perception.

The mind is your most influential creative tool. It perceives and judges situations and people based on your past experiences. There are many different perceptions on everything from the best cars to drive, to the best place to vacation, and even to what causes diseases. There is your perception of a situation, which of course must be wrong if it doesn't match my perception, which of course might be considered absurd from your grandfather's perception of the same exact situation. There are those who tout conspiracy theories, others are neutral on every issue or topic, and others feel compelled to shower you with how things really are—according to their perception, of course. What do all one of these have in common? Judgment. The symbols of words are meaningless in eternity. For us in the physical form, they are a source of judgment that clouds our perception.

Master the art of perception. This is the absolute point of all change and growth. It is only from the place of perspective that you can determine the meaning of your life and the world around you. Flex this muscle daily, first with a deeper awareness of what your perception is. If that's working for you, change your perception, and you will get glimmers of a new life. Once you begin to make small shifts of perception or shift completely, you allow for new experiences to come into your life. You might say, "Well, I don't really want new experiences. I want things to stay the same. I don't like change." But change will come whether you want it. Welcome it or resist it, it will come. Don't you want to feel like you were directing the course of change to some degree in your life? Wouldn't it be easier to embrace changes if you knew you set the wheels in motion for those changes? Mastering the art of perception is truly a gift to your self—your higher self, who knows which perspectives will create the best outcomes for you.

Insightful perception helps you to create changes so you aren't completely caught off-guard or unprepared, as we often are when we live on autopilot. So how do you do this? First and foremost, recognize when your mind is making judgments about people or situations. When you hear the voice in your head start its rantings, notice that it has occurred. Just noticing that you are being judgmental is a great first step.

Second, redirect your focus. Start by choosing a part of your body to focus upon, such as your solar plexus, an energy center in your body. It houses a lot of nerves and emotional reactivity. To refocus your thoughts to your solar plexus, you can use a soothing word like *calm* or *quiet* to restore your body's harmony. The solar plexus, also known as the Manipura chakra, the third chakra of the subtle body, is the energetic reservoir of personal power. Although this is what works for me when I need to refocus my perspective, you can focus anywhere as long as it's away from your mind's chatter. This breaks the stream of thoughts about externals. Meditation is certainly something that can help you to begin to exercise and cultivate your new ability to change any judgmental perceptions.

Our perceptions can be based on our family's beliefs, our own individual experiences, and the social influences of the time. They are usually very well grounded in the past. Whether they are blurred or clear, we often defend these perceptions passionately, despite what others perceive.

Acceptance and understanding are two important insights for changing perception. The mind and its whirlwind of thoughts have amazing creative power for better or for worse. Enthusiastic thoughts can lead to a desire for and a better ability to create a more peaceful and harmonious life for yourself. Acceptance is a knowing that the circumstances in your life are unfolding for your truest benefit and well-being. Understanding is knowing that the body, the mind, and the spirit (soul) need to be in alignment in thought, word, and deed for the process of creation to be manifested.

You can really start to work on the issue of perception when you realize that all states of mind reproduce themselves—that is, a happy thought begets a happy response or additional happy thoughts. The old saying "Misery loves company" reflects the understanding that all states of mind reproduce; they magnetically attract others who are feeling the same way.

Expectations are the foundation of resentment. It is an enormous waste of time and energy to be in conflict or to hold on to anger and resentment of any kind. It hinders the connections with Spirit while creating dis-ease in the body and mind.

Do for others out of a desire to serve, with no expectations, and you will receive the same. If you expect something in return or give yourself personal accolades, there is already resentment in the act of doing. It's no longer serving another; it's serving the self, serving the ego.

Life is an experience we chose to have as an incoming soul. It's the effect of a decision made between lives long ago. It's not a decision made alone; it was literally well thought out, like a lucid dream the dreamer chooses to dream. It wasn't a decision made with fear or angst, but with joyful anticipation of the experience ahead. There was a knowing that whatever the outcome of the experience, the soul would awaken in just a seeming instant to resume its spiritual formlessness and essence, and to reunite with the fullest expansion and unity with all that is.

I believe this experience we call life can easily be compared to a stage; we are the actors in this grand play. We review the part before we accept the role. We chose our fellow cast members, and with their agreement we participate in our many different roles throughout this physical plane. We encounter love so intense the energy could illuminate the sky, and we encounter the depths of pain and sorrow so dark we find a reason to seek faith and connection with our souls and our Source.

The roads we travel are varied and unique to our life circumstances. For me, the meaning of life is profound in its simplicity. Sometimes we make it much more complicated than it was meant to be. We chose the life we come into in this physical form to have the most joyous and fulfilling experience. When we chose and accepted this life, we did so from a place of knowing—knowing that we'd return to the Source, the Oneness. We're here to remember—to remember our true selves. We're here to balance old karmic ties and wounding and also reap the rewards of the good we've done in past incarnations. And no matter how misguided we appear to be now, in this life, most of us have all done wonderful, self-sacrificing things in previous lives.

Perception is the main determiner of how your day will go, how your year will go, and how your entire life will go. It is the justifier of how you will interact with others or react to them and your environment. In the end, it's your judgment of yourself and others and how you handled the reactions. If you allow your perceptions to be inspired by compassionate ideals and a desire for peace and happiness, which is what we are all ultimately searching for, you'll recognize whether your reactions and responses are moving you closer to that feeling or further away.

What do you feel? If you feel good and joyful, you are functioning through inspired perception. If you feel annoyed or outraged, you are further away from the peace and happiness you seek. If you can identify your feeling, you can assess your perception and change it to work for you.

Perseverance is a component of a healthy perspective. It's your will and your determination to achieve something in the face of doubt and obstacles. How badly do you want something? How quickly do you succumb to an obstacle, doubt, or delay? This is your measure of perseverance. Do you hit speed bumps and think, *Oh, I will never achieve this or that* or *Why doesn't anything ever come easily for me?* These are cloudy perceptions that will only hinder you. You must change your perception about what you can achieve and how to consciously reach the full potential within you to do so. If you do that consistently, you'll notice that you move closer to your goal instead of further away. Persevere with a new perception, and life will unfold magically.

As a therapist, I'm continually challenged to help people uncloud their minds by helping them change their inner dialogue and what actually comes out of their mouth. It can be mildly irritating to absolutely scary to hear some of the negative things people fixate on. I must always take into consideration where the person is at emotionally and on a consciousness level. I've had the great privilege of working with people who have created magnificent outcomes in their lives, but also individuals who have created disastrous outcomes. I do all I can to redirect the downward direction of a clouded mind.

The downward spiral seems to happen faster than the upward one. One unexpected outcome can turn someone toward manifesting more unwanted events just because of the feeling the dialogue in his or her mind creates. Getting people who are inherently negative to change their perspective is no small feat.

Recently, in a session with a woman in her early thirties, I recommended that she check out Louise Hays's website to do some affirmations and visualize better outcomes for her life. She came back the following week looking unhappy. "Do you really believe in that stuff?" she asked. My response was "Of course I do. I live it and breathe it every day." I gave her some examples of how my life had changed and encouraged her again to read or seek uplifting spiritual ideas to improve her mind and change her perspective on her life and why she was in this world. I can plant a seed. It is up to her to nourish it and nourish herself. Only when she changes her perspective from "my life is too hard and filled with obstacles" to "I know I can achieve anything with a little effort and a lot of enthusiasm" will her perception of what she can achieve, and of the limitless potential for her life change.

Although I believe that happiness is ultimately an inside job, sometimes it must be cultivated through the external world in which you live and perceive. Happiness must be practiced. There are so many potentially stressful things in our lives that it is easy to get stuck in a habitual pattern of negativity or melancholy. But their power can be reduced if we consciously seek states of consciousness that counteract the negativity. Happiness can become just as simple to manifest as negativity and unhappiness are.

You must first be aware that you are in a negative state and then learn to catch yourself early in the stream or loop of negative thoughts and perceptions. The shift happens with the awareness, and that same shift helps you begin to form the new habit of happiness. How is this shift made? It comes first from the awareness that there needs to be a shift then by practicing happiness activities. Smile at people when they walk by, even if you don't know them. Read a funny book (Janet Evanovich writes books that make me laugh out loud.) Compliment someone, and his or her response of happiness will be contagious. Helping another is always a good way to help yourself be happier. Make happiness your habit!

If you want to be a good drummer, you must play the drums ... often. You must practice baseball if you want to be a professional baseball player. Regardless of the desired skill, diligence and effort are required to acquire it and to perfect it. Happiness is no different. Practice happiness activities every single day, and you will achieve a happier state of being. You may also begin to notice that those around you are happier. If you're radiating light and warmth, those who are in the dark and miserable will either start to see there's a better way of being and tap into your light or they will drift away from you.

Have you ever noticed when you're tired or carrying around little frustrations or annoyances that every little comment someone makes can be perceived as something to take personally? There are times when I'm much more susceptible to catching the discontent of other people around me. The most risky time for me is if I'm not implementing spiritual practices during my day. Meditation, walking in nature, reading something spiritually reinforcing, or spending time with my dogs are all activities that help me stay spiritually conscious and connected.

I have quite a few potentially negative influences around me at any given moment that I could allow to suck me in, or I can remove myself from them. It's most important for me to reconnect to my inner happiness and joy through silence and retreat. Silence and solitude are as healing for my mind as being in nature or walking my dogs.

> There's a great little prayer in chapter 5 of *A Course in Miracles* that helps to quiet the mind chatter for me. You may find it useful when you're sick of sitting with discontent. "I must have decided wrongly, because I am not at peace. I made the decision myself, but I can also decide otherwise. I want to decide otherwise, because I want to be at peace...."

What quiets the negativity for you? Take some quiet time to identify sources of happiness, joy, and laughter. Keep them nearby for quick access. Learn how to develop a thicker skin so that you aren't offended by every little comment or slight of others. Clean up your neighborhood—not the physical neighborhood, but the neighborhood of your mind. Toss out the old clutter and pollution and toxins. Identify the thugs and move to the other side of the street; let them walk on by as you say a prayer for them and know that they arose from some distant past. Send a silent blessing, recognizing the oneness of us all. Plant happiness seeds all around the neighborhood of your mind, and infuse them with the nourishment they need to bloom.

You have now cleaned up the neighborhood of your mind. Don't allow people to walk through and throw down their trash. At the end of the day, remember that the external source of happiness has passed, but the feeling is there within to tap into. Recognize that happiness is an inside job. Practice, practice, practice!

# The Ego

A man asked Gautama Buddha, "I want happiness." Buddha said, "First remove 'I,' that's Ego, then remove 'want,' that's Desire. See now you are left with only 'Happiness.'" Buddha

Humans, unfortunately, have to contend with the likes of an entity called *ego*. The ego doesn't like to be wrong, criticized, judged steamrolled, confronted, or admonished. It sometimes acts as a victim and often acts as a bully, which is really a masked victim. An extremely unhealthy or fragile ego is in perpetual fear of annihilation and is ever on the defensive, seeking ways to cope with uncertainty. Often this looks like jealousy, unreasonable anger and resentments, insecurity, isolation, perfectionism, addictions, controlling and intimidating or manipulative behaviors. Sometimes it comes out in rage and acts of physical violence.

Reliving the past over and over again is the ego giving you ammunition to use against yourself and others, which in return keeps you a victim, making it difficult for love to enter. Victims tend to be very angry people. *A Course in Miracles* poses the question "Do you know how many opportunities you have missed to gladden yourself?" My answer is "Millions!" The ego is a powerful tool that makes us look like we're lashing out at others, but the boomerang effect applies in its impact on the perceptions of the ego-made self.

Ah, the ego. We need it to help our development and to survive in this physical incarnation and life, but then it builds momentum and it becomes the "I," the "me," the "mine." Like orphaned children, we develop the ego in response to separation from our Source. We're far beyond the veil, where there is only timelessness and certainty, and in this physical birth we are far from what we knew when our souls were merged with all.

Most spiritual teachers address the issues of the ego in their various teachings. In both *The Power of Now* and *A New Earth*, Eckhart Tolle discusses the ego in all its pathological disguises. No matter if it is an overconfident one, a traumatized one, a fragile one, a power-fueled one, or a seemingly normal one, it's still running chaotic tapes and messages through our mind in the form of thoughts. The thoughts then propel and or compel us to react, respond, or retreat.

Rarely do we look at the negative and anxiety-producing thoughts and call them out of the mind to the reality of their lies and fabrications. Instead, we assume truth from them based on fear and our past conditioning. If you look closely, you may notice, if you are awake, that most of our unhappiness is not created by situations but by what our mind is saying about them. It's created by the chatter in our head, old tapes that rewind and replay over and over. As Eckhart Tolle states in *The Power of Now*, "Such dysfunctional thinking strengthens the ego, but it weakens you."

Recall a time when you were feeling angry, self-righteous, or jealous. Did it feel good? Probably not, but the ego wouldn't let you off the hook. It probably kept suggesting all the reasons you were entitled to feel the way you were feeling. After all, you were right to feel that way because of what was done or said to you, even though in your rightness you were miserable.

Now recall a joyous moment, an experience of happiness, peace, and love. Doesn't it feel better to remember that? Then why do so many of us live in the space of the previous negative memory? It's as though we're held hostage by our own mind.

Pain and suffering happen to each one of us on some level or another throughout life. Life can be very traumatic for people. It's interesting, however, that each of us reacts differently to traumas. Someone can have severe traumatic experiences and be paralyzed emotionally, mentally going in and out of hospitals, taking all kinds of medication, truly suffering, while another person endures the same experience and he or she goes forward and has successful relationships and careers, and is relatively content. What is the difference? Why has one person been better able to move through the traumas and one has a harder time? Neither is right or wrong. It's just a matter of how their perceptions are benefiting or harming them.

One mayconsciously decide that the experience will not define his life (maybe he had a great support system), and the other clings (Buddhist concept) to the idea, the anger, the victimization, and then the suffering. The suffering then takes on a life of its own and creates feelings of depression, anxiety, and anger.

Nameless fears and anxieties often propel people's lives into directions that seem to negate their free will or detour them from their divine contract, delaying them—maybe for another lifetime—from meeting their initial karmic goals. Buddhism's Four Noble Truths recognize that there is suffering and then identify the cause of *all* suffering as the clinging of the mind. Clinging is the ego, which intersects for me in the wonderful teachings of *A Course in Miracles*. I'm always fascinated how all of the great spiritual teachings can blend and say virtually the same things.

Throughout this grand play of life, we move with a purpose. It doesn't matter whether you believe that or not, or whether you ever come to truly understand what your purpose is. You have opportunities to learn the lessons and reap the gifts of what each life has to offer you. For example, you might have been born into a life of privilege, so you must face the lessons taught you by the desires of the material world, the potential for loss, and the fear of losing the wealth and the material exhibits of that wealth.

If you were born into a life of poverty and struggle, your lesson may be acceptance and how to avoid suffering due to feeling a sense of lack. Poverty doesn't always have to mean suffering any more than wealth is a guarantee of joy. Suffering is a mental state always self-inflicted by not accepting every moment, circumstance and situation for what it is and desperately wanting it to be something else.

I know this suffering well. Reliving the past over and over gives sufficient ammunition to use against yourself and others, potentially creating a lifetime of suffering. Remaining in a mind-set of a victim prevents love from entering. Suffering may have within it the learning of nonduality and teaches us to accept the gifts of others to aid them in their own life. When those of material wealth truly reach out to the impoverished, a wonderful heart blending can emerge. All of the universe must be in balance. The poor can learn to accept charity with grace, and the privileged can learn to be charitable with compassion.

Imprisonment of the mind brings about much suffering if it is imprisoned with the body. The body can be imprisoned in jail, in illness, in disability. But only our thoughts can imprison our minds. We have within us an innate and perpetual freedom that gives the mind the momentum to move the body in certain directions, down certain life paths or to be motionless and stagnant. An imprisoned body can have a very free mind. People who spent years in prisons, such as Nelson Mandela or Gandhi, or in the prison of a body, such as Stephen Hawking, have often gained peace and insight while their bodies were imprisoned and even abused.

Insanity is often the pathology of genius. It is the truest demonstration of being a hostage to one's own mind and thoughts—thoughts of a thousand ages whirling and spinning stories and images of fantasy and fear, of power and servitude, of rulers and victims. Yes, the mind is so powerful a creator it often can't distinguish its truths from fables. It relives the ancient past over and over in an attempt to correct perceived wrongs and prevent future offenses. It doesn't recognize its own game.

The main rule of the game is to realize that most thoughts are lies. We can't seem to erase old tapes and automatic negative thoughts, despite the pain and misfortune they can bring. So why do we even have the capacity to think at all? Maybe it is to gain mastery over something that's both primitive and divinely inspired. Our task is to go into the silence to understand the meaninglessness of most of our thoughts and the profoundness of what *is* profound and therefore meaningful. The free mind can hold you hostage to never-ending negative thoughts or peaceful and content thoughts. The awakened mind helps us choose the outcome we want to experience.

At those times in life, when we feel it necessary to rebel, the mind seems to have no ability to implement a buffer before reacting. That may mean that we're much more easily angered than usual, because we quickly interpret everything as a threat to our ego. Or, to rephrase that, the ego feels everything is a threat to it and reacts. Above all else, you feel that you must assert your ego in your own highly individual way. And if you've been unconscious of the need for creative change in your life, you're likely to be quite explosive. Sometimes, however, the explosions happen to you, which is a sign from your environment that you need to break away from something, although what that is may not be at all obvious or, worse yet, too terrifying to face.

Most of the time, our most intimate interpersonal relationships are the perfect soil for sowing the seeds of our soul's growth and truest desires. The interactions don't always feel good, but they're always significant. People trigger parts of your personality that need healing and are separate from the person who triggered them. If you don't look at that wounded part of you, and you can't figure out what your reactions are based on, you will reunite with it again when another person, relationship, or situation triggers it.

All people have wounded parts of their personality, their selves that are brought into all of their relationships. Whether it's with their children, boyfriend, girlfriend, spouse, or sibling, those wounds are either worked out, integrated, and healed within the relationship or enhanced, and rewounding or an added wound may occur. In the past, I found it to be at times mildly annoying and at worst painfully depressing trying to match my personality with someone else's. Sometimes a sense of powerlessness rose up, and I was left to wonder what was going on in my life. Now, however, I'm better able to reach for a different perspective in most situations.

It's so much easier to look at external factors and people—and in my case, significant others—and say, "Well, he has issues" or "He had issues" or "Oh yeah, that one really was messed up." But the thing they all had in common was *me*. This isn't to say they didn't also have their own wounds that I triggered; they did, and I did. It's in the attempting to merge these wounded humans together for work or play or intimacy which isn't easy. It always erupts when one or both haven't been healed of these wounds or shattered parts of their human personality. The soul, however, is always in perfect unity and love.

The greatest and most difficult lesson is to realize who you really are. We are not the small little "I" that judges others and resides in distrust and fear. We are all, each and every one of us, powerful and eternal spiritual beings who, when given the right emotional environment, are innately joyful, happy, loving, and compassionate.

I believe that the personalities we have taken on are also a chosen aspect of our earthly incarnations. They were chosen as the way to provide our souls the most opportunity for growth and evolution into higher consciousness. However, you aren't your personality, despite the frequent use of its traits to describe you. The people you love and hate aren't their personality, even though they may have an intense impact on you. Someone might describe you as funny, generous, miserly, loving, workaholic, lazy, dependent, suicidal, melancholic, or joyful; this serves you as you meet the challenges and merits that go with having such a personality.

Some people you love immediately; some people you want to get away from as fast as possible. That's the vibration that specific personalities convey and generate. It's only the masks our souls wear to move us along. In reality (mine anyway!) our true essence is who we are based on all the lives we've lived and all the lessons learned—well and not so well. We are our most ancient and deepest joys and darkest nights and fears, remembered by our souls and expressed in our behaviors, our relationships, our life circumstances, and our personalities. It's like a compressed zip file; we can open the contents, but it takes knowledge to access the database. Sometimes we're successful in accessing the truest parts of ourselves, and sometimes we just can't seem to get out of our own way.

We may often experience days that feel heavy, weighed down by our vast sea of changing emotions and thoughts, weighed down by the mind and its endless chatter about all things "me." I have experienced sullen days because I've allowed myself to get sucked back into the mind chatter. It's funny how our thoughts can create sadness where there is nothing really happening that is sad. Once that happens, the challenge is to release them and get on with the day.

Unfortunately, for many of us it isn't always easy to do. We all have similar dialogues playing out in our minds, day after day and year after year. Wishing for what isn't, rejecting what is, hoping for the thing event (in my case, it's the lottery) that will give us the freedom to pursue what truly makes us happy. Many people struggle with going to their jobs daily, thinking "the boss doesn't care about me or what would make me happy" or "I wish I could enjoy life personally and professionally." With everything we believe we want or need to give us happiness or peace—whether it's a new car, a college degree, or an ideal romantic partner—we're really longing for the feeling that these things might bring.

An ideal partner may be your desire and then you manifest that in your life only to find out your perception of an ideal partner has changed. Then you have another feeling. For some, the material thing is a new home. The feeling underneath owning a home could be pride. It could also be a sense of worthiness, safety, or just fitting in or belonging. Unfortunately, when these objects are no longer live up to our expectations or fulfill the duties we have placed on them, our lives are easily propelled into fear, anxiety, or chaos. The loss of control over these people or statuses might then change our feelings from "I'm okay and I belong" to "Oh no, now what will I do?"

We so often think, *If only I had more money for [fill in the blank], I would be very happy* or *then people would like me better*. We believe that if we have more money, new things can happen or happiness will come. In some cases, this is true, but not for most. I personally know that money won't make me happy, but it would sure make life a little less burdensome and busy. There's an obvious need for money, but the extent to which we strive and work to get money can lead us to forfeit relationships, leisure, and creative, spiritual, and joyful pursuits. Very often we even sacrifice our health.

I've been poor, and I've worked hard, and I enjoy a relatively comfortable life now. But the time for joyous pursuits to enjoy deeper spiritual practices retreats and to see new places is all wrapped up in having time, free time.

This is the issue for many of us, time is never free. It always comes with a cost, the cost of doing and the cost of not doing (working for a paycheck). *Free time* is the oxymoron of the twenty-first century! The idea of be/do/have has become do/have/be. We of course have it all backward.

What are you sacrificing in pursuit of more money? What would be the worst possible outcome if you were to lessen that pursuit? What would be the greatest gift?

# Mindfulness

A mindful mind is precise, penetrating, balanced and uncluttered.
Bhante Henepola Gunaratana

Inner peace leads to outer peace, not the other way around. One person at a time can create peace internally. He or she can then act from that place, quietly sending out a peaceful energy vibration experience to one other person, who may give it to his or her family, who will bring it into the community, which may uplift an entire city. Everyone has access to this divine inner peace, even when things in life suck. We can still achieve inner peace and harmony through understanding that all emotional states that lead to suffering are temporary and through accepting each one in the moment.

I understand the pain and suffering that comes from wanting circumstances in your life to be something other than what they are and feeling like you can never get to where you want to be. It can be overwhelming if that wanting of what isn't and rejection of what is starts to suck you in. You do have a choice either to keep suffering or to stop suffering. It may be hard to accept that there is a choice when one thing or another is "happening to" you and it is unwelcome. This choosing requires great mindfulness and isn't easy. It requires, first and foremost, a deep awareness that you can make a different choice, a choice not to feel pain and suffering. Though this isn't easy, it's the only method likely to bring about a better state of mind.

Enlightenment in my experience takes a lot of practice. Some days you may feel very enlightened, and then, a few days later, feel like you couldn't be any less enlightened. Personally, I've found it to be a process instead of an event.

Although some people I've read about had instantaneous awakenings, such as Eckhart Tolle and Byron Katie, few of us have an instant epiphany. Sure, it's easy to attain some level of enlightenment (meaning transcendence from the mind and thought) while sitting alone in a cave for a decade or living a relatively cloistered or monastic life free of the mundane interpersonal stressors and burdens that plague our lives as society greets us each day.

When you have to interact only with an occasional bat, snake, or insect in your cave or meditate with other cloistered aesthetics, it's easy to remain mindful and peaceful and at one with creation. There are no real surprises, and any slight disturbance is easily remedied. True enlightenment comes when you reach that state while being fully involved in the day-to-day tasks and conflicts of significant others, coworkers, and children who may irritate you by not meeting your expectations.

Angry people crossing our path or any of a myriad of interactions that happen to most of us every day cause a perceived need to respond, react, or initiate a situation. Oh, what I wouldn't give to live a semicloistered life in close communion with nature with just a few kindly people and some dogs to fill my time. The mind chatter would certainly slow down, and the activities of the world would lose the level of importance and urgency I place on them. A knowing that all life is unfolding in harmony with the Source of all creation and that there's no need to force outcomes would evolve.

Screeeech ... but wait. I have to go to work, to the grocery store, to the wedding. It's almost back-to-school time, and on and on it can go. So, what are we to do? We do actually have to go to work to buy the groceries and to pay for the back-to-school clothes and supplies. How can we achieve a higher level of consciousness, if we chose to, while locked into the daily grind? Part of the answer is initiating mindfulness and checking our motives often. Checking motives means really being honest about why you feel compelled to do something.

For instance, some kids outgrow their clothes in two months; they may actually need new clothing. Maybe. But some parents have another subconscious agenda; they want to make sure their children have what the other kids have so that Mom's ego doesn't suffer from envy and jealousy. Or Mom may succumb to the ego of her teenage daughter, who has to have this or that, or she'll be horrified to walk into school in the same clothes she had on 2 months ago. The quick remedy for that is a little trip to West Africa, where they dig holes outside to use as a toilet and where there are no designer bags or shoes or makeup.

Of course that isn't possible in most cases, but this extreme example reveals something many people lack: gratitude. A basic willingness to give and to help others enables you to receive much from others as well. People can sense whether you will conduct all your transactions fairly. When you demonstrate the ideal of integrity, they'll be fair with you as well.

People stay confined in their little lives in little routines that cause them to develop more fears of the unknown, so they don't move. Their comfort zone shrinks down smaller and smaller until it is so small that the big fear of death keeps them from living. It's as though fears decay their minds. Then the vicious cycle goes on as the decaying mind causes more fears.

A decay of the mind has submitted too long and too deeply to the whims, desires, and tactics of the ego. Relinquishment of decaying thoughts becomes more difficult over decades of misuse. Relinquishing those thoughts, however, is not impossible. Think of changing those thoughts as self-correcting. If you continue to reach for the highest, the best, and the kindest thought in every situation, be it large or small, slowly your mind learns to perceive and think differently. With each successful shift in perception, the decaying of the mind slows and then reverses to a more pure and more loving higher awareness. From one single thought to collective thoughts, we establish the power of intention in a more universal way.

I've asked many people what they believe happens when we die. I'm still surprised when someone says something like "We just go into the ground and become worm food." Some say things like "It's just lights out" and nothing else exists. Little do they understand that it's just the opposite. It's lights on!

In the field of addiction, the disease model is the most widely supported. It is sometimes a challenge to help someone integrate the idea of a spiritual crisis. People have responded with statements such as "Are you saying I made myself get this disease or I wanted this?" Of course that's not what I would suggest. It's easy, especially with addiction, to incorporate or embrace the disease model. I've heard people say they're mad at God. I understand where the statement originates from (a fearful mind), but God doesn't put alcohol or drugs in anyone's hands.

Thankfully, as people get sober and participate in therapy and twelve-step programs, they begin to be more open to the spiritual part of the true nature of dis-ease and recovery. They change their perceptions about how they came to be addicted to a substance in the first place. Both the disease model and spiritual ideals are critical to the healing process in the beginning. The awareness of the spiritual crisis is necessary for healing at that level.

All healing comes from enlightenment. Keep in mind that healing is not the same as cured. Enlightenment is a shift of perception to knowledge that the true self is connected to the All that is healed and healthy. Deepak Chopra discusses this in many of his books and teachings, stating that healing, health, and wholeness all come from holiness. Many people also with depression receive enormous benefit from spiritual healing and intervention. Some seek it out, and some stumble on it through their own recovery groups and therapists.

Depression happens for many reasons. Some people prefer the belief that it's a chemical imbalance, and in some cases, that is likely. For instance, many individuals with bipolar disorder truly have chemical imbalances. But for depression and anxiety the source of the suffering is at the level of the mind. At the core is clouded perception and judgment and also an unconscious feeling of disconnect from a spiritual center or guidance. I don't mean going to a church or another place of worship. Yet I've noticed there is a common theme among suffering people: they have lost or rejected their awareness of their connection to their Source. Often they're isolated from family or friends, leaving them feeling isolated and resentful.

When there is that disconnect on top of having tried to get sober or not be depressed over and over again, it's almost easier to blame God. Unfortunately, not looking at the distorted mind and perceptions and seeing them for what they really are allows them to manifest as pathology, disorder, and disease. I believe the real core is the longing of the soul to remember its connection to Spirit, to God, to the place of creation, to being free and light. We have an unconscious yearning to be unencumbered by the physical life and the earthly trials and tribulations of the body. In the book *Sufism*, this is described as "the limitless ocean of longing."

All conflicts are of the mind, even though there are bodies involved or bodies being attacked. There's no exception to this. *A Course in Miracles* teaches that even when bodies are reacting to either an illness or an attack, the conflict *originated* in the mind. Therefore, the *correction*, the *healing*, the *release*, and the *resolution* must also be at the level of the mind.

Once a perceived emotional or physical injury occurs, the mind starts a mental dialogue. In the early stages of trying to change your perception and release the mind from clinging, you might notice that no matter what form of relief you seek—whether a physical activity or a different mental activity—it's as if your thoughts are attached to a bungee cord, always trying to pull you back into a place of suffering. Being mindful of your breath and having a compassionate heart are the best practices for ending the clinginess of your mind. They are much better than letting your mind lead you to despair and worse suffering. Breathe in loving kindness; breathe out righteous indignation.

If you're feeling low or depressed, intentional activity is needed to raise your vibration and bring about a better feeling. Believe that every feeling you feel is a choice. Initially set your focus on a thought about something, and an accompanying feeling will come. If it's a happy feeling and you continue to embrace it, you have chosen happiness. If it's fear or anger, you'll have a thought that corresponds to that. It's your choice if you want to hold on to it. All thoughts and emotions are included.

Grieving is probably the toughest emotion to shift. Losing a loved one can create great depths of sadness. It's always beneficial to seek support from family, friends and even bereavement groups for help. Another challenge we often face is learning to let go of grudges and grievances. When I was younger, I could hold grudges for ages, and I still never forget anything. However, holding a grudge is different from remembering. A grievance against someone for what he or she did to you in the past can trigger fear and anxiety in the present. I've learned that I don't like that feeling at all. When I'm aware that it has come up, I have a choice to return to the old grievance and continue to fuel my grudge with more old thoughts or to turn it around quickly. I reach for compassion quickly. There is no need to delay in this, but we do. We feel entitled to mull over whatever wrong has occurred and ruminate on why it shouldn't be.

You can try something different. If you can, forgive the offense immediately. If you must, give yourself permission to mull for a specific amount of time, such as one hour. I wish I could say that I'm a speedy forgiver all the time. I let go of grievances with much less residue than I ever have. I haven't perfected it yet, but I'm much better. I'm almost always stunned when I find myself upset by some old issue that I was certain I had overcome. It pops up again just to remind me I still have some work to do.

Overall, however, I no longer hold on to grievances for months or years, letting them fester to resentment. I still have moments of annoyance or, at worst, righteous indignation, but I'm better able to move past something in a few minutes or a few hours. I do know for certain that whenever I "sleep on it," I'm relieved of the unpleasant feeling. The dawn of a new day breaks the chain of frustration or anger or sadness. It changes my perspective. Through being more mindful, I can see clearly the trickery of my own mind. Then any negative dialogue of my mind is quieted.

This seemingly new-age concept of mindfulness, which is actually ancient, is a conscious shift of perception. Mindfulness can be initiated with an awareness of what is commonly referred to as the golden rule, or the ethic of reciprocity: Do unto others as you would have them do unto you. This is found among all the world's ancient and modern religious and spiritual teachings. The Quran says what is hateful to you, do not do to others. Confucius said, "Never impose on others what you would not choose for yourself." The ancient Egyptian Middle Kingdom had the saying "Now this is the command: Do to the doer to cause that he do thus to you." Ancient Greeks said, "Do not do to others what would anger you if done to you by others."

My favorite version, from Isocrates (436–338 BC) and found in the many readings of Edgar Cayce, is "what you sow, so shall you reap." I get that fully. I remind myself of it daily. I've seen it and experienced it in both beneficial ways and not-so-beneficial ways. Now I'm much more in tune with that, and I choose accordingly. I'm aware that what I sow, I *will* reap, whether it's tomorrow, next week, ten years from now, or when I cross over. I check my motives and my agendas before I make a particular choice. I'm aware of where my thoughts are going, and I call them out when they start going in a direction that makes me feel suffering. I often say aloud to myself, "That's a ridiculous thought. Stop it."

Be conscious of your divine essence, your true self—and create your physical earthly life from that place of knowing. All the characters you've invited have arrived, or they're on their way. Be joyous in anticipation of the blessings each one brings to you. Await not your tiny version and vision of perfection and perfect timing. Each moments is a perfected interlude between you and your Creator, who watches with love and wonderment as you join with him to create true perfection, leading to the ultimate merging with him.

Don't buy into the fears and uncertainties that the ego places before you. Rise above these obstacles to free yourself from those boundaries. Once you change the scope of your vision to one of expansion, you'll see that nothing is beyond your reach.

# Manifesting the Good

*"Every thought you entertain and accept becomes a part of you and will inevitably bring you the physical reality of your image."*
Uell S. Andersen

Nothing is beyond the ability of your thoughts and feelings to create and manifest. I know this to be true. If you could consider that everything that has happened in your life started with a thought, you may be open to learning the art of manifesting consciously in your life.

The mental dialogue that plays out in our minds has power. Like a magnet attracting steel, your thoughts and the feelings you put behind them lead you to take certain steps in certain directions, for better or worse. Look around at your life. What have you created? Are you happy? I don't mean, are you happy that you have a Mercedes or the Harley you've always wanted? Would you be happy even if you lost those things?

Can you see that the link between what you want and what you get is all from the seeding of thoughts? I consider myself to be a great manifester. About a year and a half before I sat down to write this book, I'd wanted to start a private psychotherapy practice. I didn't know how I could do it with the hours I worked at a hospital and the additional financial burden I believed it would require. I already had the name of the practice: Thrive.

A good friend offered me free space to share with her as a start. Although it was very generous, our scheduling overlapped, and I couldn't get to that place. Then my boyfriend noticed a sign for office space at the bank we use. I'd called the number several years before but never followed up. This time

I did. The landlord generously decreased the rent, so the first gift of the universe was a price I couldn't refuse.

I'd put out there that I wanted an office either at my home or close to it. The building is three minutes from my home. Additionally, it's on a lake. The energy of the water and the bank, which are important to be near because water raises my vibration and a bank means money, made it the perfect space for a psychotherapy practice called Thrive.

Right after I signed the lease, my significant other texted me an "OMG!" message. While he was putting air in his tires at a local gas station, he noticed something not too far off on the ground. It was a music CD by a Christian music group called Casting Crowns. The name of the CD was *Thrive*! True story! (Check out their home page, CastingCrowns.com.) I'd never heard of them. The first song was also "Thrive." I took all of those as signs from Spirit that I was on the correct path for my venture. I bought some furniture on credit, and now, only a year later, I have a thriving psychotherapy practice—so much so that I was able to fearlessly drop a day of work (and pay) from my full-time job to continue to sow the seeds of my future.

Another validation from Spirit was through the landlord again. As he was preparing the office for me, he asked if I wanted it to be painted a certain color. I told him yes and said I liked greens. He said he would paint it off-white, and I could paint it green if I wanted. I agreed.

About a week later, on a Sunday afternoon, he called me to say his wife had found a gallon of green paint and he had started painting. He asked me to come to look at the color. My living room at home is two-tone green; the darker part is sage. I love that color—and the office wall was painted sage green. This may not seem like a huge manifestation, but it was another validation from the universe that has helped my confidence grow. I was able to move one step closer to fulfilling a dream with each synchronistic moment.

Each time you dismiss an idea, a creative impulse, or a change and hold on tight to avoidance, procrastination, or fears of the unknown, you may miss an opportunity for growth not only in your current circumstances in the physical but also in your soul. Fortunately, patterns and opportunities do repeat themselves and are likely to show up again as part of an evolving manifestation. I would rather attempt something great and fail than attempt to do nothing and succeed. What good is empty success?

What is your dream? What would you like to manifest into reality? Believe in your own ability to achieve anything. Spirit is close at hand, helping you along your way. Don't be afraid to invest in yourself and your dream and then see how magnificently your life unfolds.

# Time

> All real progress in the long history of humanity is marked by milestones of truth erected by its devotees along the highway of time.
>
> —*Edgar Cayce*

In this world, we are often at the mercy of time, almost paralyzed by our perception of it and our management of it. We fear its end and believe there's never enough of it to get us through.

*A Course in Miracles* discusses time extensively, including this statement: "Fear is not of the present, but only of the past and the future, which do not exist." If we were to apply this statement and have a consistent awareness of its meaning, it would leave no place to be afraid of what lies ahead in an uncertain future. There would be no regret of the past that holds you in bondage and servitude.

The past can't be undone. Yes, you can learn from it and make the experiences that brought you joyful outcomes useful, but there's no benefit in carrying around the rest. You can assess the past based only on the present. Projecting worry and worse-case scenarios keeps you afraid and stuck. The future, which doesn't even exist yet, rarely plays out as horribly as we have dreaded or imagined. Only in the present do we realize how wasteful the emotional toll of projecting negatively was and how it was just the ranting of a clouded mind.

The illusion of time was a gift given us to be used as a tool to manage useful happenings and assess our growth and other worldly experiences. In the world unseen, where we all ultimately return in an instant, there is no time. Freedom from time allows for the instantaneous manifestation of a thought. In that realm or dimension—or whatever word you feel most comfortable with for describing the spirit realm—a thought *is*. For example, a thought of the Taj Mahal can instantly bring you to the Taj Mahal. A thought of mother brings you to mother. There's no delay in the manifestation, because there's no density of form or time.

Thankfully we do have a delay in manifesting thoughts here. Time keeps us from overload and keeps the universe in order. Imagine every one of our wishes, needs, and desires all showing up instantly. That would cause worse chaos in the world than there is now.

We are all "doing time" in one way or another.

Those unfortunate enough to be doing it behind prison bars and walls are just doing it under a different set of circumstances than the rest of us. In our human incarnation, regardless of our level of awareness, all of us are living in a time-bound realm. The difference between here and the hereafter is time versus timelessness.

Timelessness is the true essence of the term *eternal* with regard to the spiritual dimensions. The teachings from *A Course in Miracles* emphasize that time is an illusion. For those who are reaching for and nearing an unclouded mind, the knowing of the eternal and timeless life hereafter can be glorious and filled with anticipation and joy or frustrating as our desire to be home deepens.

As your spiritual awareness broadens, you begin to understand on a deeper level what the life experience is really about for *you*. It's different for each of us. For some, the abundant life experiences may be focused on enjoying the bounty of Mother Earth, Gaia. Many look to balance out their own karma and not make any bad karma while they're here. Others have a desire to be done doing time in the physical. Buddhist teachings describe this as the desire to break free from the karmic wheel of Samsara, which is ending the cycle of rebirth. For others the time is used to gain personal mastery in some area of life that wasn't experienced very well in a previous part of the soul's journey. How each of us uses our time here is assisted by the gift of free will.

The benefit of the still clouded mind may be that there is no awareness or anticipation of what awaits in timeless realms. Some people spend their days watching the clock as they work many hours a day, dreading each minute until it's time to leave. Some people make every effort to live joyously each day without being straddled by time.

Try to recall when you were sixteen years old. If you were like most of us, you thought you would live forever. You may have reminded everyone that you were almost eighteen and would then be considered an adult. At that time in our lives, we often reject suggestions to get certain things done, believing we have an endless amount of time to do them. Then fast-forward fifty years, and time has a very different and more significant meaning. An elderly woman who realizes she's nearing the end of her life may desire more time to make her children dinner or see her grandchildren grow up. The perception of time between these two souls is very different. One believes he will never run out of time, and one knows her time is running out. The remedy for them both is the same: staying in the present moment, knowing truly this is all we have.

Time is very important to most of the world. For instance, a specific group of people is fully aware of time: individuals who are in recovery from addictions. They're often keenly aware of the time they have clean and sober. In self-help groups, such as Alcoholics Anonymous, some say that the time sober isn't important. Others say when you work hard to get clean time, you see its importance. They're both right in their perception of time for themselves. On the flipside, if too much emphasis is placed on that time, and if they relapse, it's more difficult for them to return to sobriety. Their perception of the importance of time convinces them that they "lost the time" that they were sober. In this example, time can be burdensome.

Many individuals I've worked with who have spent years addicted or years incarcerated express a desire or need to "make up for lost time." By staying in that mind-set, they waste more time in regret. "Lost time" was of the past, and you can never redo it. In believing that you can only creates more suffering and more missing of the present moment. Time is a gift to some and a burden to others.

As the saying goes, we're on "borrowed time." Some of us borrow more, some less. People struggling with terminal illness or who are near the end of their life often wish they had more time. Those who suffer with chronic pain, whether emotional or physical, often wish for freedom from their time-bound body.

I've had the privilege of working at a hospital for the past eighteen years, and I have the utmost gratitude that the universe has aligned me with this job. It has afforded me great opportunity and growth. Recently, however, I was feeling like I had absolutely no time to enjoy the home I pay a mortgage on or to spend time with my dogs, my significant other, or my mother, who just turned seventy-three. So I put a little message out to the universe, asking for a reduction of hours without hardship or fear.

Six months later, I was given that gift: the gift of time. I was permitted another day off a week. I've enjoyed being off three days a week, with two days off in a row, for the first time in about thirty years. I've discovered that the gift of time, for me, is more precious than money. At the end of this physical life, the money doesn't mean anything for any of us and often even less to those closest to us. Most grieving people wish for another minute or another hour with their loved ones. They say, "How sad she is gone," not "Where is their wallet?" (Notice I said "most people." Of course there are a few who care only about money.)

Time can be wasted, lost or precious. It can feel like an eternity of misery when we're required to endure something we don't want to do (like the treadmill for forty-five minutes), but it goes by much too quickly when we're having fun. We grieve the past, we fear the future, and we miss the present. I think the majority of us, when we come to the point of assessing how we've spent our lives will have some regrets that we didn't have more fun, love better, and stress less.

Sometimes you must be willing to give something up in order to receive something else of far greater meaning or significance to you. I've read numerous stories of CFOs and CEOs of large companies who make salaries that would make the wealthiest individuals gasp, decide to walk away from all of it because they had no free time or they weren't happy or to pursue a long-held dream or new idea.

Some people stay at jobs they hate for twenty-five years, and are miserable but too afraid to leave because of the fear of not earning the money and losing the time already invested. Some women at the pinnacle of their career, success, and financial abundance just want to be stay-at-home moms. Some men reach the highest ranks in corporate America and walk away to be able to travel the world. I can almost hear the gasps of shock and disbelief of those who spend year after year working and still live paycheck to paycheck. These inspired individuals tasted the success that many of us want, only to find out that it didn't fulfill the expectations of making them happy.

Only when you're doing something you truly love and feel passionate about will you feel fulfilled. Imagine a woman who has an important position or lucrative career—earning all the money she needs to give her children anything they might need—walking away from it. This has happened often. When she does leave it behind, it's likely she's feeling her spirit's true urgings.

In many of these cases, all the women wanted to do was spend time with their children, helping them to reach their milestones or just being there to make the best peanut butter and jelly sandwiches ever. I can imagine that for each of them those activities were much more purposeful and joyful to their soul.

Often we're restless. This feeling is an urging from our soul to do something specific that is our unique calling and purpose. The man that leaves his job as a CFO of a large international company to take pictures of the wildebeest migration in Africa or grizzlies in Alaska is looking to tap into his adventurous spirit, his truest self. From that can come great bliss and awe of the world around him. The gifts he may share as a result will be much more meaningful, more inspired.

Recently my best friend, who is very artsy and creative—she can design interior spaces like a pro—decided she needed to "get a real job." So she trained to become a pharmacy assistant/technician. She breezed through the training and landed a job with a large company quickly. Unfortunately, that large company had small cubicles. After spending nine months with her eyes glued to three computer monitors, having virtually no meaningful interaction with coworkers, she peeled her eyes from those monitors and resigned.

You can't squeeze a soul looking for creative expansion and glorious experiences in their earthly life into a cubicle. To thrive, she needed more meaning and all the joyous experiences a lifetime can bring.

The incarnated soul gets to experience time, form, and humanity instead of its true home of timelessness, formlessness, and eternity. Although the passages through each of the spiritual levels or bodies do not necessarily have a time-based correlation, our cumulative lifetimes are akin to the spans of hundreds of earth years, maybe even thousands. Many of us are battle-weary old souls who have experienced violent eras in history. As we move through this time-bound life, one of our biggest human challenges is dealing with time. We watch it tick away all day long, month after month, year after year.

Trying to fit a lifetime into any day is impossible here. The demands of family, work, and self pull us in so many directions that it sometimes seems impossible to make heads or tails out of which way to go. When I feel hurried or pressured by mundane and necessary tasks of life, I remind myself of my true timelessness, and I make a conscious decision to expand my consciousness and remember my true home and truest eternal self. Grounding myself and breathing properly helps me achieve this.

Trying to stay in the now is easier said than done when you have to show up and be accountable to various people. That's *my* biggest challenge. I crave the freedom to embark on any earthly adventure I choose without worrying about the mortgage and the credit card bills and the boss.

We experience time here as linear. There is a past, a present, and a future. There are things we have to do now and tomorrow and next week, and some things we didn't get a chance to do yesterday. For instance, I started writing these ideas and thoughts for this book about seven years ago. I'm just now creating the sacred time to get it all into a book format.

Spiritually speaking, time doesn't exist. It's a concept that came with the separation from our Creator. It's a necessary part of this experience called life. Without it, nothing would get done, and our whole purpose for being would come to naught. Our lessons here in this life rely on a clock, which allows us to measure our accomplishments and set our goals.

When I had my first past-life regression, in May of 2011, I had a very strange experience of timelessness. As I discussed the details of what I was seeing (I was an American pilot flying over the ruins of Germany), I had no awareness of how long I'd been at that deeply relaxed level. When it was time for me to come back to the present, I thought I'd been under only about ten minutes. I thought it must not have worked very well, because the therapist was reorienting me so quickly. Unbeknownst to me, three hours had passed.

What is the real difference between time and no time, or time and eternity? What if your life, as the old song goes, "is but a dream." Imagine that in the course of a lifetime, whether it's eighty-two years or nine years or one day (all of which *are* lifetimes for that soul), at the instant of death you find out you were only Anthony or Elizabeth for a millisecond, an instant, a blink of the eye.

Then imagine that this is true for everyone, no matter how old they are, what they did with their lifetime, what their ethnicity was, or what religious or spiritual beliefs they had. Not even how they left the physical body really matters, except to those left behind. In that instant, they are as free and unencumbered as they were before they entered this life for this life experience. The only thing that really matters is whether they were kind, loving, helpful, and compassionate. Did they live from that place, or were they unkind, showing little or no compassion, a hostage to the defilements of the ego.

As with the snap of the fingers by a hypnotist, you will awaken from the illusion of being that body or that personality with a specific name and set of life circumstances. You are instead all that you could ever think, feel, and be, with absolutely no obstacles, fears, or doubts. Everything you think *is*. Every thought manifests instantly, because there's no delay caused by time and matter. When you are awake, you will know that the entire experience was just an illusion.

Why would we choose to have a hypnotist put us "to sleep"? Simply for the experience. For all of us who sleep at night, there's a potential for happy dreams and fearful dreams. Once we awaken from sleep, we quickly realize that the experience was only a dream. This is also life.

In my meditative practices or deeper quiet states, I try to tap into that timelessness. By quieting my mind, being in silence, walking in nature, or connecting to nature on some level—even if it's just sitting on my deck, listening to the birds or the crickets—I can find that place of calm and peaceful abiding. This is how I nourish my spiritual self. When I need a rest from the daily grind, I often read spiritual books that remind me of my true self. Meditation is crucial for my sense of comfort and peace; solitude is as sacred as the air I breathe. When I don't take the time to meditate, I can feel irritability rising and can become frustrated by circumstances or impatient.

I am unbounded by time when I go within. I can step through the veil to timelessness, temporarily leaving the mundane.

Doesn't your life impart to you certain joys? You believe you're restricted by your perceived *bindings of time*. To free your *self* of this perception takes a glimmer from the amnesia, a breakthrough if you will, to remind you that there is no binding that matters or holds you, in eternity. Those perceived bindings of time hold you only in physical time and only if you choose to be held by them. You were created with *boundlessness,* with the universal Source's intention of unlimited *wonder, awe,* and *joy.*

Try to use your time consciously. Consider and observe the many potential paths you could take. Then you'll see that absolutely anything is just as possible for you as for those who have already achieved it. Know that the time of your life is now and that you can move forward with confidence or stand still out of fear. You *are* in charge of how you use the precious gift of time.

# Beyond the Body

Under every physical cloak … I am.
Whatever the hats I must wear or the roles I must play,
They can never conceal, I am. Whatsoever my personality perceives of itself,
However grand or diminished, it can never diminish or undo I am.
When all is peeled away, and decay sets in upon this body,
I will always know
The eternal, I am.

—Laura Chiusano

Beyond the body is a world unseen by the eyes, voices unheard by the ears, lessons unlearned by the mind. Beyond the body, our true home awaits, as does the Source of all existence for all of time and eternity. Beyond the body, the breath of life is quieted by the brilliance of light. Beyond the body, there is unlimited expansion of thought and manifestation. Beyond the body, the universe is completely unobstructed by matter and form; vision expands to understanding.

One of the biggest questions that nearly all of humanity longs to know the answer to is "What happens after we die?" All cultures and religions address this question in their sacred texts. Ancient philosophers, and more recently new-age thinkers and metapyhsicists, explore the question and present their insights and perspectives on what they believe happens after death.

The reasons for birth into physical incarnations are interwoven between the worlds. The main goal is the soul's desire for spiritual ascension and full merging into oneness with the Source. The path taken is determined in part before birth, and then free will allows for self-direction. In this use of *self*, I'm referring to the personality rather than the spirit or soul of self. Imagine that you decided to go to sleep for a while, and when you awakened, you realize you have had amnesia and you start trying to figure out who you were, who the people around you were, and what you were doing there with them.

After we leave the body, most of us continue to have a strong affiliation with it from the other side. We think, *Oh, that's me, but it isn't me.* There may still be a strong link with the personality that has been left behind, including all of its worldly affiliations, such as religious beliefs and ethnicity. However, that need to identify the self as the body diminishes as the soul reacclimatizes to its truest essence of self—the eternal self rather than the temporary "me" of the physical body.

We have had many "me's" throughout our physical incarnations and journeys. Some of those me's we'd just as soon forget and some we hold dear. They are all significant and meaningless at the same time. That can sound very confusing, but if you can accept that each life experience is significant for that soul's growth yet unimportant to the eternal nature of the soul, you're closer to understanding what we are all doing here. This doesn't mean bad deeds go unacknowledged. There is cause and effect in the ethereal realms just as there is in the physical realms.

We travel through many different levels of consciousness both in the body and beyond the body. We ascend or descend depending on what we seek to gain mastery over from life to life and between lives. Yes, there is activity between lives! When we're beyond the body, learning happens through accessing all the spiritual levels with the help of our guides, higher beings, and soul mates. There are many different levels or realms beyond the body. You reach the level that's most appropriate for your soul's growth as you do when you return to another body. The unconditional love, guidance, and wisdom we receive builds our spiritual confidence to go on to the next level to assist and help others with their lessons. We're always given the opportunity to help another soul as we are also being helped.

This topic is one I can discuss all day and read about endlessly. Life beyond the body includes things such as near-death experience, spirit communication, awareness of kamma, and the various planes of existence. It also includes reincarnation, which is referred to using several other terms, such as metempsychosis, rebirth, and reembodiment. Many religions support the belief in reincarnation, but they refer to it in different ways. Buddhists believe in rebirth of the spirit as karmic memory and transmigration of the spirit to many different bodies. The purpose for them is to achieve freedom from Samsara, which is the continuous cycle of birth, death, and reexistence, rebecoming, or kamma to more lives and incarnations. The end of that cycle is a purified state called Nibbana or enlightenment.

Many people cringe or reject the notion of reexistence, reincarnation, or any kind of rebirth. Interpretations of religious teachings may deny that such a thing can happen. However, all of life is reincarnating all the time. On a cellular level, our organs and bodily systems do this regularly. Seasonally, trees die off, dropping their brown leaves, and flowers wither away into dormancy only to be reborn the next season, the same but different from year to year.

Similarly our souls await the right season to return for their growing. Unfortunately, some suggest such a concept is blasphemous. That biblical teachings were written down over 2,500 years ago, in the language of Aramaic, and translated many times into many different languages escapes people's rational mind. Therefore, they respond with fear to any other perception than the literal meaning of the words.

Imagine the telephone game, which often plays out in life. For example, you call a friend and mention your frustrations about your job and how you have a conflict with someone on the job. You express that you're feeling tremendous discontent. Then you interject some if-onlys into the conversation: if only I didn't have a mortgage, I'd definitely quit; if only my wife wasn't unemployed; if only I didn't have to pay my kids' college tuition, I wouldn't stay at that job." Then you end your phone conversation.

However, your discussion gets a second wind in the form of gossip—not malicious, but nevertheless gossip. Your friend starts telling his friend that you were so unhappy at your job that you were resigning. That friend relates the story to someone else who adds that you had a verbal altercation with a coworker and were confronted by your boss, and "I think he was asked to resign." Now imagine conversation being revisited by someone who doesn't speak fluent English. To suggest that the gist of the conversation may get lost in translation is an understatement. In light of this, consider how odd it is that translated ancient religious teachings are accepted as infallible.

Now throw in a little ancient history. The Romans—yes, those controlling ancient rulers—decided that many of the interpretations of the Bible were too permissive to keep a society in compliance. So what did they do? They took out anything that let people know they were loved unconditionally and that no angry God was coming to strike them dead and that there were no literal fires of hell. And furthermore, any mention of something such as reincarnation was blasphemous and could bring about death as a punishment, regardless of the fact that there were many references to reincarnation in the Bible. So it remained a secret wish and belief not often spoken of except by the philosophers of those eras who had a distinct insight and knowing. They too were forced to mask their words so that they were in accordance with the laws of the time. Thankfully, some discussions that were left behind survived and found their way to modern times.

Some Bible verses refer to reincarnation many times. One passage is Matthew 11:13–14:

> "'Why then do the scribes say that Elijah must come first?' ... He answered them and said, "Elijah indeed is to come and will restore all things. But I say to you that Elijah has come already, and they did not know him, but did to him whatever they wished. So also shall the Son of Man suffer at their hand.
>
> "Then the disciples understood that he had spoken of John the Baptist." (Matthew 17:10–13).

Jesus stated the following, referring to Elijah, whose story can be found in the Old Testament:

> "This is the one ... there has not risen anyone greater than John the Baptist. ... And if you are willing to accept it, he is the Elijah who was to come. He, who has ears, let him hear" (Matthew 11:11–15).

The life of Jesus of Nazareth was not the first incarnation of that soul. The first was Adam; Jesus of Nazareth was the last. He is an ascended master and has no need of another incarnation. He built upon previous incarnations and achieved perfection in his final incarnation. His previous incarnations were numerous and, according to mystics and clairvoyants, such as Edgar Cayce, he had previous incarnations as Jeshua, Asaph, Joshua, Melchizadek, Hermes, and Adam, just to name a few. The Epistle of Jude (14) in the New Testament states, "And E'-noch also, the seventh from Adam, prophesied of these, saying Behold, the Lord cometh with ten thousands of his saints."

Although I've always believed in reincarnation, my interest in it grew enormously after reading *Many Lives, Many Masters* by Dr. Brian Weiss. I was astounded by what his patient Katherine could recall. So I read book after book on reincarnation. Reading *Journey of Souls and Destiny of Souls* by Dr. Michael Newton inspired me to have a past-life regression. I was also interested in being able to utilize past-life regression hypnotherapy in the psychotherapy practice I was still manifesting in my mind.

One of my hopes for having a past-life regression was to find out who and why the people in my life were here. I found out a tidbit in the first regression, but it wasn't until three years later that I was given an opportunity for a bigger glimpse through Dr. BrianWeiss.

During my first regression, I found that I was a man in a past life not too long before and that I'd flown a plane over Germany. It was weird, as I could see the rubble of a city beneath me. I ultimately wound up on an aircraft carrier, leaving England to go home to Iowa or Ohio, I believe. During the course of that regression, I saw that I had a small daughter who died at the age of four or five. In that lifetime, I ultimately became an alcoholic and died in a quarantined tuberculosis ward.

The crazy part is that I've never had any interest whatsoever in war movies or war history, so I didn't know that one could go from Germany to England and then to the United States on an aircraft carrier. I also had never seen what a quarantined TB ward looked like. I googled a picture of it after the regression, and it was exactly what I had seen.

A friend of mine who was very excited about the regression immediately found the name that I'd carried in that lifetime and found that he lived in the same state and was predeceased by a young daughter. I was very surprised, to say the least. In this lifetime, I chose consciously not to have children, and I work with alcoholics. Thankfully I haven't had any health problems like TB.

*Life after Life* is a great film by Dr. Raymond Moody, a philosopher, psychologist, physician, and author. Moody has investigated thousands of near-death experiences (NDEs) and cases of people recalling past lives. This particular film recounts several individuals who have had NDEs and how every one of their lives changed afterward. In fact, two of those individuals were believed to be so dead that they were in the morgue when they returned to their bodies. In fact, one man returned to his body during his autopsy!

One individual discussed her NDE, which came as a result of her attempting suicide by shooting herself in the chest. She didn't die, and during her NDE, her guides gently advised her that if she chose to stay on the other side and "die," she would have to have another lifetime experiencing similar circumstances and pains that led her to attempt suicide; she would also have to find ways not to commit suicide again.

Suicide breaks your spiritual contract, so to speak. There's no way to walk away free and clear from a difficult life. Because you leave behind piles of pain and suffering for your loved ones, there is a karmic cause-and-effect due to such a decision. Your souls are here to grow and experience life to its fullest. A perception of suffering leads to such a sad decision, which can't be undone. The woman, who did this to herself chose to live. She wisely decided she didn't want to have to endure another hard life. She knew that she wasn't alone and that she was loved unconditionally. Her NDE changed her life in that she felt love and compassion for herself and others and knew her existence had deep meaning.

After their NDEs, all of these people knew that they weren't their body and that there is an expanded consciousness beyond the body. It was a challenge for them to readjust to the life experience again. If you're struggling to believe or accept that there is much more beyond the body, I encourage you to get that film. The individuals sharing their experiences are not actors. They are sharing their stories.

As a therapist, I encounter many people who are suffering or having difficulties. I always try to help them find deeper meanings in their experiences and I try to find more meaningful ways to assist them. Often this means thinking outside the therapeutic box. Early in my current relationship, my significant other and I went to a past-life regression workshop hosted by Weiss at the Javitz Center in Manhattan. I was so excited to be there, in the front row, to have whatever experience would come.

William was interested in the experience but hadn't read *Many Lives, Many Masters*. He was open to the experience and fully embraced past lives and past-life regression.

Weiss began the regression with a relaxation meditation. He then directed those attending the workshop to recall childhood experiences from this life. As he moved through the regression, he guided the attendees to recall their in utero time and then finally beyond this life. I wasn't having any past-life experiences, which was very frustrating for me. It was even more frustrating when I looked over at William, who was in the emotional grip of a past-life memory. He tearfully "returned" with the details of what he'd experienced, both visually and, clearly, emotionally. I quickly moved beyond the indignation of my ego to listen to his amazing experience, which I've shared just as he wrote it immediately after he had it.

> 1800's Laura and I lived out west in the Plains States. It was just her and I on our ranch. We were settlers expecting our first child. Laura's name was Alice and she was in a very light blue dress. There was a doctor who was there to deliver our child. I was outside by a woodpile and a split rail fence, leaning on the split rail fence. I heard commotion from inside the home. I was outside with my border collie named "Scout" who had a bandana on his neck. I heard Alice scream and then there was silence. Scout started barking as the doctor came out to get me. Both Alice and the baby died at child birth. It was stillborn - inside her womb. The doctor had blood all on his clothes and I wanted to hurt the doctor. Scout was still barking. It was chaos. I was very distraught and the doctor was very apologetic. I lived on the ranch with scout until I died of a disease from that time era. I floated up out of my body but was very upset that Scout would be by himself and felt I was abandoning him. I wouldn't let go of my earth body as I wanted to be with Scout. Finally a spirit conveyed me Scout would be fine and it was time for me to be with Alice and our baby. I felt free.

We knew we had some previous lives together, but this was in such vivid detail for him, it was amazing for both of us.

If you can find someone who does past-life regressions, either in a group or individually, it is well worth the investment. Healing of a great magnitude may occur. Physical and emotional well-being may be restored, and harmony in relationships may be improved. I've read many stories of family conflicts being played out, creating chaos and hostility. Then one person went for a regression and gained an understanding of why the conflict was playing out.

One such story was a mother and daughter who absolutely couldn't get along. The mother admitted she didn't like this child but had no ill feelings toward her other children. When she had a regression, she found out that in a past life, she and her daughter had been rivals for the same man. That man was the husband/father to these women. The mother didn't share this information with her daughter, who later went to have her own regression done. She unveiled the same lifetime. This immediately improved their relationship; they were able to move past it and resolve the karma (cause and effect) from that lifetime.

## The Unclouded Mind

Credit for the most recent level of fearlessness for me goes to a woman named Anita Moorjani. I haven't met her yet here on the earth plane, but the experiences she had and wrote about have helped me to release a lot of useless fears. She had an NDE while dying after a lengthy struggle with cancer. Despite having done everything she thought she could to avoid getting cancer, she got it anyway. After much treatment, both traditional and holistic, the end was apparently near, and she lapsed into a coma. In her book, Dying to Be Me, Anita shares the details of her NDE which included the experience of being in different places simultaneously. She witnessed and heard conversations of doctors and family members, some of whom were not even in her hospital room. She was able to feel the emotions that her family members were feeling. During her NDE she reunited with her father who had died several years before as well as her best friend who had died from cancer. They were there greeting and encouraging her. She was given glimpses of such beauty and knowingness that we are all perfect and one, that our words could not fully express her experience. When she awoke from the coma she remembered everything and was anxious to share it with her family and then ultimately the world. Her experience was a gift for all of us.

Whenever any of the old fears or anxieties creeps back in, I remind myself of her experience. Many other sources have reinforced for me everything I've believed and known about the afterlife and beyond the body.

For a brief time, there was a television show called *I Survived ... Beyond and Back*. I looked forward to watching it and hearing personal accounts and reenactments of NDEs and how they'd changed people's lives. Not one of them said their life worsened. Once people have the opportunity to see life from that very different perspectives, their lives are never the same. One case was that of a neurosurgeon who had discounted NDEs as real—until one happened to him. Doctors are first and foremost scientists, and if it doesn't add up in an equation or a hypothesis or some other scientific proof, it isn't real. Dr. Eban Alexander also wrote about his NDE in his book called Proof of Heaven. No longer the cynic, he travels extensively sharing his experience and providing comfort and inspiration to many.

One day I was sitting on my deck, enjoying a beautiful May day. It was sunny, and the sky was a deep blue. There was no sound, except the chirping of birds and the trickle of the fountain in my little koi pond. As I was gazing up at the few little clouds passing by, something strange and exhilarating happened to me. I was in such a state of deep relaxation and peace, I felt an expansion of my true self stepping out from beyond the body of Laura. I truly felt the oneness of everything; I was part of the billowy clouds, the sun, and the deep blue sky. I felt like I disappeared for a minute but to somewhere blissful.

Immediately after that experience, I wrote the poem in the beginning of this book, "Impermanence." I felt I had a deeper understanding of impermanence. I knew that the other realms were accessible for each of us under certain circumstances.

I spent days trying to reach that sacred space again, just to get another glimpse, because it felt so freeing. I've never reached that space again, and I wish that I could daily, just to hold on to it and feel and remember the knowing I felt. But as is the law of impermanence, this experience passed. It was just a small glimmer of something I can only describe as a brief lifting of the veil, and I wanted more of it.

"Wanting more" is the true experience of the "clinging" described in the Four Noble Truths. I can only imagine that there may be the desire to experience the oneness, liberation, and expansion that Anita Moorjani, Dr. Alexander, and countless others who've had NDEs probably long to hold on to in every sensory way possible. This is why they must share it with the world, so that we may vicariously become part of that experience; it keeps the experience *alive* and nearby for them.

We all have fears and anxieties about some things in our lives. Some individuals even have paralyzing fears than others. I've had some barriers in my life due to fears that limited me in some ways. Or, in reality, I limited myself because of them and then it was just a vicious cycle. Although, in all of my massive amounts of reading, I hadn't come across anything I didn't believe and felt certain of, reading about Anita's NDE impacted me the most

*The Unclouded Mind*

at a time that was most beneficial to me. It was reinforced through my heart, where I actually needed it, and I've been able to use it and benefit from it instead of my ever-so-analytical mind. Now, when those around me cling to the safety of their beliefs, which are often contrary to my own newfound fearlessness, I can better protect myself from their negative influence.

After reading Anita's story, *Dying to Be Me*, the first time in 2013, I decided to go to a five-day training workshop to learn past-life regression therapy with Dr. Brain Weiss and his wife, Carole. The workshop is held at the Omega Institute in Rhinebeck, New York, twice a year. I'd had a page from the Omega catalog on my kitchen cabinet, on the wall at my office, and on my bedroom mirror. I knew I could manifest my attendance, even if it was sold out. I looked at those pages every day for over a year, though I was reluctant to spend the money for the workshop and the five-day stay at Omega. I also wasn't sure how I would get there. My driving had been limited to Long Island.

I attended even though it was sold out when I'd registered, and I had been number 150 on a waiting list. I drove upstate all by myself quite fearlessly. The day I arrived at Omega, my cell phone died. I knew I had to get another phone before my trip home. So the next day, on the lunch break, I ventured out into the world and found a Verizon store, following the direction of Omega staff. The nearest one was in Kingston, twenty-five minutes away. It was pouring rain. I mean *buckets* of rain. Thankfully GPS was at my side. It took me right to the Kingston Bridge. Did I mention I had also been afraid of bridges? So there I was, in the pouring rain, driving over the longest bridge on the planet, as far as I was concerned.

At the Verizon store, I was stunned to hear a woman tell the clerk, "Did you hear we're under a tornado watch?" Yes, a tornado! Thankfully I made it back to Omega without being scooped up and whisked away to the Land of Oz. I don't believe I would have left Omega to go to the Verizon store in the pouring rain in a place I'd never been if I didn't read her book. In fact, I may not have gone to Omega at all.

Things quieted down, and I was able to get on with the training. During one of my regressions during the workshop with Weiss, I unveiled a life I had in the AD 52. I was in Crete and saw my other self, a male on a white, horse-drawn chariot. I had or was shown (I'm not sure how to describe it) a chunk of thought about slaves, and this is what I wrote:

> People don't understand what it is they are here to learn. As the Masters, one must not be harsh with their slaves, lest they will be returned as such to those they mistreated the next life on. In that lifetime I was murdered with a boulder to the head by someone who was angry that I suggested treating slaves better. Why that would come as a memory, I have no idea, but it was fascinating nevertheless. There were several other regressions and experiences. Nothing was life changing for me as a result, except the experience of having done it, which just fueled my interest in it more.

Once I was home after completing that workshop, I felt like there was nothing I couldn't do. I'd changed my perspective on driving beyond Long Island and on investing money for my own betterment and enjoyment. As a result, I met many new people and, of course, the Weisses. I stepped out of my comfort zone and went beyond the body.

As a psychotherapist, it isn't always easy for me to quiet the thinking part of my mind, but I'm mindful of that and work on balancing analysis and imagination. This is important for all of us, so we can blend the creative with the thinking for the most fulfillment. Trying to be rather than do is more of a challenge for some, while others spend so much time just being that not much gets done.

I've given *Dying to Be Me* to many people, and I encourage at least one person almost every day to read it. I've recommended it to my clients and people in my personal life who are being held back by fear. One of my clients, who was preparing himself for the death of his ninety-two-year-old mother, was struggling somewhat with how to handle that process. Even though he is a very spiritual man and has a belief in a happy afterlife, I was still sad that he had to prepare to say good-bye to his mother. We miss the ones we love when they cross over. He read *Dying to Be Me* and found it to be so useful that when he went to see his mother for the last time, he read some of the book to her. She responded with a sense of peace to the following excerpt regarding Anita's NDE:

> After my NDE, things got a whole lot easier. I no longer feared death, cancer, accidents or any of the myriad things that used to concern me ... except for expanding out into the greater world. I've learned to trust the wisdom of my infinite self. I know that I—along with everyone else—am a powerful, magnificent, unconditionally loved, and loving force. This energy flows through me, surrounds me and is indistinguishable from me. It is, in fact, who and what I truly am. (128)

When he pointed this section out to me, it took on a whole new significance for me—so much so that I taped a copy of the entire section on my mirror and in both of my offices. It's a borrowed affirmation that I read daily, a reminder for me to stay connected to my true self. I also encourage clients who are struggling with low self-esteem or anxiety and depression to read it.

Unfortunately there will always be cynics and naysayers who reject and attempt to refute these experiences. Ironically they do so out of fear. People who are grieving yearn to know what happens when we die; it gives them comfort to know that their loved ones aren't lost to them forever and that they still have the bond of love.

The fear of dying is one of the biggest we humans carry around. But when people say they had an NDE and speak of the unconditional love and reunion they experienced, they are often perceived as oxygen depleted or, worse, spiritual cons out to make money writing books. It's unfortunate that, over the centuries, people have become so narrow-minded about spiritual and metaphysical experiences. There is so much potential healing for all of us, if we all could embrace it.

People can't even bear the thought of their death or the death of loved ones. They're terrified by the very mention of it and find it all very distressing. Death, however, doesn't really exist. It is just a stepping out of what I like to call the "flesh suit." If you've seen the movie *Men in Black*, you may recall the entity known as Edgar taking off the "Edgar suit" and unveiling his inner alien. Well, that's us. We are walking around in this suit that cannot be eternal and will inevitably decay and rot. What's left is not at all alien, but pure divine consciousness—a fully incorporated sense of knowing what your life experience was about and then returning to that divine expanded consciousness where you reconnect with all that you left while you slept. Death is what happens when you're busy making other plans.

Experiential knowledge, of course, can never be known in life except through those who have had a near-death experience and returned to tell us about it. I feel strongly that those individuals had their NDEs for me and for everyone else open to hearing about them. Live from that place of knowingness. It is very liberating.

Many writers and metaphysical practitioners have described crossing over as a graduation. That makes sense for beginners on the spiritual path. I see it as awakening to my true self once again. Death isn't something I fear, because it doesn't exist as the finality that the word conjures. I know without a doubt that the afterlife is timeless and unbounded. Whatever I don't get a chance to experience on the earthly plane is always only a thought away and at my soul's beckoning when I cross over.

What do you believe happens beyond the body? How does that belief shape your life? If it creates fear in you, investigating spiritual teachings and ideas is a way to release that fear. I have always had very vivid and lucid dreaming. Not long ago, I had a dream of an older woman speaking in an open-air auditorium filled with people at a lecture I was attending. I have no idea who she was, but she said, "When you believe that God takes people from life at the peak of their lives, you diminish the truth of God. That is your opinion; it is not the truth of God. The light of God should never be diminished by worldly opinions, and it cannot be." Then she said amen.

I believe it was a message for those who have lost someone at a young age. It was a brief dream that seems to fit right in with this writing and with what I believe to be the truth. Those left behind may never accept the passing of others. We miss their presence; we long to feel their physical body or touch them in some way. Because it's sometimes difficult to see the bigger picture, so to speak, the pain can be debilitating for years. When you can embrace the purposefulness of their life and their return home for their soul's growth and know they are only a thought away, acceptance can begin and so can healing. Hopefully knowing that brings comfort.

In this lifetime, I've had to say good-bye to friends and family members that have crossed over. Although I miss people, and especially my dogs, I look forward to the moment I cross over and see them all again. I know it will be as though we've never been apart. However, there is a huge caveat with that statement: Death is not up to you. There is an enormous spiritual price to pay for taking your own life or being reckless with your life or someone else's.

Spiritism is the belief and acceptance that life in Spirit goes on and that those no longer in physical form can be reached by channels or mediums. There are many mediums among us, even if we don't know it. I believe every person who has lost someone should go to a medium at some point in the grieving process. There are many good mediums, and there are many ways to access them.

There's nothing like the healing validations that come from beyond the body, from your loved ones who have crossed over. They provide enormous comfort that they are still with you and accessible to those who can perceive at a different vibration. Francisco Cândido Xavier, a famous Brazilian writer, spiritist, and medium, wrote many books in collaboration with André Luiz in spirit. One of the statements made in their book *Action and Reaction* (1956) was "if incarnate souls could *die in the body* only a few days every year, not like a physical sleep during which they recover, but with full awareness of the life that awaits them! Yes that would certainly change the moral face of the world."

There is another reason Spirit often comes through a medium: to offer glimpses of the world beyond the body. I've sought out many such writings and read many. One such case, of which there are thousands, was spirit communication between a man who was alive in the physical body. His name was Anthony Borgia, and the spirit who started communicating with him was in life Monsignor Robert Hugh Benson. The monsignor died in 1914 at the age of forty-two; he wrote the book *The World Unseen* through Borgia. To summarize, his spirit came through to make right the incorrect teachings he had left behind as a Catholic priest. He wanted to share what the afterlife was *really* like. His guides helped him bring the communication through to Borgia, who was clairaudient.

I could write an entire book on this fascinating type of collaboration. *A Course in Miracles* came about in the same way. Mediums and channels exist all over the world. For example, João Teixeira de Faria, better known as John of God, lives in Brazil at a place called The Casa. Through his devotion to God, he became a medium for healing. Spirits known respectfully and lovingly as the Entities come through him to heal those who are suffering with illness of mind, body, or spirit. These many entities were doctors in their earth lives and have continued to heal millions who pilgrimage to Brazil or seek them out when John travels. I have been fortunate enough to be one of those people. In October of 2014, John of God and the beloved Entities came to New York. They are hosted by the Omega Institute as are Weiss and many other teachers and healers.

William and I spent three days there and were in the direct presence of John of God and the spirit of Dr Augusto de Almeida. The experience was a very deeply spiritual one for me and for many who attended. I believe that during those three days, over three thousand people passed before him. We were privileged enough to be taken with about twenty other people to a tented area where John spoke about how he does this work, giving all praise and thanks to God. He tearfully expressed his gratitude and humility for the Entities, who use his body to do the healing work.

This is an exhausting endeavour that João takes on every day of his life. But he never complains; he just loves unconditionally every soul that passes before him. The Entities that come through him perform miraculous healing surgeries and other procedures on those who need them most. They even do distance healings. We both had a distance healing before we went to Omega and then a "spiritual surgery" while there in the presence of João. As a Spiritist he knows that there is a beautiful continuity of life waiting for us beyond the body. Don't be afraid to investigate these teachings and experiences. No matter what religious discipline you follow, there are no other-worldly sanctions (hell) awaiting you if you expand your mind to include other things.

All of this spiritual seeking and awakening has had an additional impact on me, one that some may consider a negative outcome, but I certainly don't. I have a much broader perspective and understanding about death and some of the physical and emotional health crises that people have, such as job loss or economic issues. I have great empathy for their trials and tribulations, but I can also see that all events and circumstances are for the greater good of that soul and the rest of the world on some level. Our life lessons here help us to gain mastery over some of the things we struggle with or that led to our demise in past lives. Often the opportunities for the most growth come from the most difficult or painful experiences. I tell my clients that their souls must have been ready to take on and resolve the many hardships they are experiencing.

Every day I feel like I'm walking between two worlds or two realms of life: the physical and the celestial. The sublime feeling of having a close and knowing interaction daily with the other side and Spirit is difficult to resist. I try to hold conscious contact with the glimmers I have been given of the other side, because it feels extraordinary for me to be in that space.

But sometimes it's necessary to just do regular stuff, like go to work, pay the bills, and walk the dog. I must ground myself in the here and now, while also remaining consciously joined with the other side. Sometimes it's a challenge. So we must wait and go about our life with some level of knowing that we ultimately return home to the glory of our true selves, and it is as though time never existed. We will be aware once again that everything is happening as is most beneficial for each of us. The separation we feel from those who have gone home before us will be erased as we return to a glorious reunion, as though we were never apart.

When it's a challenge to walk between two worlds, I feel a little homesickness. This poem I wrote conveys that feeling.

    Homesick

        Torn between two worlds,
        One of form,
        The other, the ethers of eternity,
        Remembering the beauty,
        Remembering the unity—
        Here there are joys.
        Here there is beauty, but sadness abounds.
        And fear becomes an earthly duty.
        We must patiently wait,
        Some of us knowingly,
        For that special date
        When remembering turns to reunion
        And life eternal rises gloriously.

Be reminded that you are still an active part of your true home and experiencing your physical life here. We are here and we are there. Open your mind and quiet yourself to receive what *creation* wishes for you at this time. Release the fears and uncertainties that prevent you from full reception of these truths, for they are already within you to access at any time.

I'd like to help you reflect upon this: The body is a vessel that carries your *soul* back *home*. It is a caravan for which your journey delivers you and your *bounty* of life experiences back to the plane of *divinity, light,* and *love*. For you *are* that divinity, light, and love. It is only a matter of choice to *believe* or *not believe*. Your light emanates bright enough to *always* be in that sacred space, regardless of your physical life circumstances. I implore you to remember these truths, for they will *sustain* you when you are feeling weary of this journey.

There is absolutely nothing you can do to be disowned or abandoned by God or Spirit or your Creator or Source. Even if you do not believe in the existence of a divine creative source or higher power, it believes in you. All of the judgments you experience are of the *ego*—yours and other egos. Though they may judge you or even harm you physically or emotionally, you can never be rejected by your Source. Your light, however dim, resonates back to him and grows brighter with each loving thought or act of *compassion*.

Feel not damned by your circumstances, for you are loved *unconditionally* and *abundantly*. You receive all that you embrace, and what you reject will consciously or unconsciously will fall away. Always seek a higher thought, a more loving response, a truer expression of your soul. Recognize the perpetual *joy* your soul vibrates at and make an effort to tap into it every day.

Planted within us are the seeds of divinity and splendor. The only thing that keeps these seeds from reaching their full potential to bloom is limiting thoughts we often carry around for decades. Splendor and holiness are our Inheritance from our Creator. They are our birthright.

Everything is truly achievable when you consciously tap into that knowing and begin to create the great life you are entitled to. Affirming that can be the beginning of having the seeds sprout and then bloom.

It's rarely easy to accept the journey we've chosen to take. In fact, it isn't easy for most people to accept or believe that they did choose to take on their specific life prior to being born. Nothing is random or coincidental in this life. We are not born to be doted upon by our loved ones, make a few happy memories, endure pain, work, pay taxes and die. In the end what would be the purpose of such a meaningless existence? There is so much more meaning to our lives beyond what the five senses can perceive. The more that I understand and experience the more compelled I feel to share about the many spiritual and metaphysical teachings I most embrace. Because they've helped me to reawaken, I want to pass the information along, like a treasured family recipe.

## Soul to Soul

> I seem to have loved you in numberless forms, numberless times ...
> in life after life, in age after age, forever.
> —Rabindranath Tagore

Our life is about our relationships. Every soul lesson is directly related to interactions with others or a lack of interactions with others. Much of what we believe about ourselves is based on some of the most intimate relationships we have. Family, close friends, and loves all contribute to our identity. If the relationships we experience, especially in our formative years, promote love and support, we will have a much different sense of self than if they were neglectful, abusive, or nonexistent.

Every relationship is an opportunity for lessons and growth, no matter how long they are or what path they follow. How we incorporate theses relationships is significant. We can have enough insight and consciousness in relationships to allow them to become our spiritual practice, or we can continue with the day-to-day conflicts that come up and react from the unconsciousness of the ego.

Spiritually, we just can't get it wrong. Nothing we do is wrong. It is always part of our path. This doesn't mean we don't feel the effects of them. In many of Edgar Cayce's life readings he often stated that in a life an entity gained and lost. No matter how one perceives any individual's life, there is always an opportunity for both. This is about cause and effect, known in many Eastern spiritual traditions as karma. Our daily encounters with others as well as with those who make brief appearances are purposeful. Those individuals we invite into our lives—be they friends, lovers, or children—aren't there as our property or possession; simply and exquisitely, they exist to fulfill their own roles and destinies. They are the soul mates we agree to do this dance with ... until the dance is over.

There will always be opportunities for growth through each of these encounters, whether we perceive them as positive or negative, loving or hateful. Seek the higher truth, and the message of love and learning will touch your soul's memory. This isn't anything new; it has been written about for centuries.

All meetings with other human beings can be perceived as useful or problematic, based on the level of intensity that the relationship creates. As *A Course in Miracles* states, *every* meeting or chance encounter is profound, not because of its intensity, but because it happens. Some people you meet are just passing through for a brief encounter, and others are with you for years and lifetimes. These relationships are all part of the divine plan and therefore all profound and important. We can be very conscious of this or not conscious, which may determine the level of impact. Some souls stir our emotions and compel us to move to and from different situations. Some stir feelings of anger and fear, and some of love and joy. The feeling tends to be the guiding force that determines the next phase of the relationship.

Most of us have had déjà vu at some time in our lives. Déjà vu is a feeling of familiarity with a person, place, or situation you know you have never encountered in this life. Usually we experience an "I feel like I did this before" moment, and then we forget about it. We see it as something we can't explain.

Déjà vu is the essence of a forgotten memory tickling your consciousness. It may last for a moment, but you might deem it insignificant among the myriad other things you deem insignificant every day. But what if it is significant in the bigger picture of this experience we call being human? Would knowing this help us to take time out of our busy lives to pay more attention or to be more conscious or kinder? Could we be inspired to look at seemingly insignificant interactions as a potentially profound and meaningful connection? Hints and déjà vu moments can hold keys to past relationships, future paths, and spiritual partners that may hold the very light we need to heal and grow this time around.

As I consider the impact of people on me, I can see the meaningfulness in each and every relationship. All interactions occur at a time when mutual teaching and learning can occur at the level the soul is ready for.

Think of the people you have the strongest feelings for, both positively and negatively. They are souls of relationships in your past. Some are from the not-so-distant past and some the ancient past. When I ask my clients to consider the idea that they have chosen this life, their reactions range from mild amusement to horror. Common responses are "Why would I choose to be an alcoholic?" "Why would I have chosen incarceration" or child abuse or unemployment and poverty? Of course they reject the idea. It's worse if I mention that they chose their parents. You would think I'd accused them of robbing a bank.

People who have lived challenging lives due to the erratic behaviors of their parents can't fathom why they would have chosen parents like theirs. They ask, "Why would I choose a mother who is mentally ill?" or "Why would I choose a father who is abusive?" It isn't easy to suggest that it was for the betterment of their soul and all others concerned combined with free will to make choices. It's not that anyone chooses a life of conflict or, worse, abuse; it's that the soul incarnates with a desired plan for its own growth and as part of an agreement to join with others to help them with their soul growth.

Individuals can respond only from the level of awareness they have evolved to. For some, it is still quite primal and guided by the hostile reactions of others and their own juvenile impulses. Remember the pendulum of life I discussed, during the adolescence of man the mind is much more reactive and dangerous. Our decisions are based not only on our level of development but also on free will. There's always a better way to go than abuse or addiction or violence to self or others. Some are just not ready to dig deeper or to release old, worn-out ideas that are no longer serving them well. That's okay. They will learn anew somewhere on their spiritual journey.

Now I have fewer clients who think I'm talking nonsense, because more are ready to hear something about past lives. As time goes by and the therapy evolves, so does their openness to such ideas. Something as simple as a coincidence becomes more to them than what they would have previously believed.

I am always seeking the deeper meaning of why people come into my life. As I became more awake and less on autopilot, I started to notice the timing and "coincidences" of chance meetings and friendships. This was most dramatic for me with coworkers and clients. Everything seemed to have a pattern, and people I met for one reason long ago would reappear many years later for no apparent reason. I used to have a "hmmm, that's bizarre" mental acknowledgement and move on—until I couldn't. I now have a deeper need to know and understand who they are to me on a soul level.

"Life is ever changing," "the only constant is change," "everything happens for a reason"—we hear these phrases throughout our lives, often in response to events that are unexplained, fearful, or unwelcome. These events, or challenges, are usually accompanied by a precipitating situation or set of circumstances. Sometimes they are created by our own choices and sometimes by the choices of others. When other individuals bring changes, we can choose either to accept or to reject those changes.

Some people are catalysts that propel us into turmoil or a change we didn't want or prepare for. Who are these people, these catalysts who wreak havoc or bring bountiful joy? Perception determines the answer for each of us. When we have wonderful experiences with someone, we like to think of him or her as a soul mate. But we also have soul mates in individuals we don't like. There are people we identify as problematic in our lives. I regarded these negative and often unwelcome individuals that flit into our lives kicking up anger and resentment as portals of pain. A portal is an entrance into something. So those we are in conflict with do not bring new pain; they kick up what may have lain dormant for years or decades.

If we associated negative experiences or emotions with someone, negative reactions that we don't quite understand can arise. The challenge is to stay mindful that they too are carrying with them residuals of the past, and they are not the identity we affix to them. Some connections are brief but still important, because their purpose is to get us to someone else or to another life circumstance. This may not be evident immediately but becomes more apparent down the road on life's journey. Although a connection can be intense and deep, it can also be painful in its intensity and potentially damaging to our life and life circumstances. None of us can avoid them for our entire life. We all get at least one, and some of the less awake souls get many more. Why? What is the point of what seems to be a negative yet overwhelming connection?

The answer again depends on what we believe and how attuned we are to our soul's purpose in this physical form. Consider that everyone you meet you are supposed to meet as part of the divine plan, whether the relationship lasts for ten minutes or fifty years. When they show up, it is the exact right time for them to show up. I know without a doubt that every client that comes to see me for therapy is supposed to at that time. I know it's the best opportunity for a teaching to take place. And this is a mutual teaching. I've learned much more from my clients than I could ever teach. I've learned that every symptom, such as anxiety, depression, addiction, or eating disorder, is directly or indirectly the result of a relationship. Whether it's a relationship that went wrong, was lost, or was never there; a longing for a relationship; or a desire for a present relationship to be different, each soul is seeking resolution. When that resolution isn't perceived to be happening, the mind suffers. We are spirit looking for connection to spirit.

Consider that a neighbor's kindness or lack of kindness is not a random life event. Or even consider that a stranger coming to your aid was an opportunity for you to learn some little thing that you were ready for at that moment. At the same time, the other person was ready to hear or learn something from you. Even a chat with someone online or at the supermarket is a divine encounter. Along the journey of life, interactions have a ripple effect somewhere at some time, whether it is a five-minute interaction or a five-hour one. Sometimes it's an opportunity to just smile and say hello. Sometimes holding the door open for someone renews the hope in humanity that he or she has lost. How would you be different if you knew there were no chance encounters?

Have you ever had an experience then stood back afterward and thought, *OMG! What were the chances of that happening?* Did it leave you wondering about the coincidences of life or at least of that encounter? If you did, you noticed divine synchronicity. My boss of seventeen years and I used to have interesting discussions about the sometimes seemingly crazy spiritual seeking that I was doing and that he had done earlier in his life. One day we were discussing a mutual interest in how we had felt a strong pull to read about something but couldn't understand why.

He was very interested in those involved in old time organized crime personalities. . He knew the stories behind many of them. I had a pull toward stigmata. I know it's strange, but I'm fascinated with stigmata and anyone who has been proven to have stigmata. Stigmata are wounds of the crucifixion that spontaneously occur, such as a spontaneous bleeding on the palms and top of hands, feet, and sometimes head, signifying the crown of thorns forced on Jesus of Nazareth before he was crucified. There have been several church documented cases of stigmata. St. Francis of Assisi, the patron saint of animals, received stigmata. In fact, he was the first recorded case. This was back in the 1200s, as he died in 1226.

One day, toward the end of the workday, Jim and I had a conversation about St. Francis and stigmata, and then I went home. A few minutes after I got home, I heard my neighbor Dominick calling me from the other side of the fence in my backyard. "Hey, kid," he called out to me. Dominick was in his seventies at the time, so even though I was well into my forties, he called me kid. "I got something for you," he said enthusiastically in his Brooklyn accent.

I looked over the fence, and he had painted a large concrete garden statue of St. Francis of Assisi for me. I couldn't believe my eyes. Only an hour before, I had been in that conversation with Jim, and I was being given a statue complete with stigmata. It was almost like I was being given a glimpse of what was happening behind the scenes.

Dominick has since relocated to Santa Barbara, California, and my statue remains in my garden, a little weathered but still holding for me the fascination of the gift and the synchronicity of the offering. Of course, there are no coincidences, and although I spent many hours and days trying to analyze the hidden mystery behind that experience, I ultimately had to just laugh at the way things unfolded, knowing it was more significant than my mind can grasp.

Even moving to my home and having the neighbors I have is part of the bigger picture. I know this undoubtedly. People disregard these things as coincidences, and I used to as well. All that changed for me one night when I pulled two cable bills out of my mailbox. It's miserable enough to have to deal with one cable bill, but two—yuck. One was mine and one was for a neighbor who had recently moved in with her fiancé. I looked at the bill and saw a very unusual last name, but it was familiar to me; it was the last name of Eileen, a dear friend of mine from my younger years. The cable bill was addressed to her uncle Bill, who, unbeknownst to me, had been living behind me for over a year. I don't live in my hometown, so it was more than just a coincidence, and I knew that immediately.

As we get older and start having our own families, it can be challenging to stay in touch. When Eileen moved, there was no Facebook, Skype, Instagram, or any other social media. Unfortunately, I had only occasional contact her, as she and her husband and children had been living in California for twenty years. Eileen was the friend with me when I went home to find my house had burned down. Her parents were kind enough to welcome me into their home to stay until we moved into another house.

A series of synchronicities unfolded, starting with that cable bill. A few years later, Eileen, who was then terminally ill with lung cancer, was brought back to Long Island to be cared for by her wonderful sister and her own family. I had the great blessing of spending Fridays with Eileen for a few months before she passed. The chain of events that allowed for me to get that opportunity to reconnect with her started with her uncle's cable bill in my mailbox. It was truly a special-delivery message for me, and if one thing had been amiss, I may have missed that time with her.

Passages through the physical incarnations lead not only to gaining information and knowledge on the physical plane but also to a transformation and an increased capacity for love and acceptance, both here and beyond the veil. The light you emanate is very dim at first, so others may shine upon you to lead you to brighten your light as well. The shared flicker of a flame enhances both.

As you move through the physical moments and instances, your light intensifies, and you become a beacon for newer souls just beginning their earthly journeys; they are ambitious yet emanate a dimmer light. You surround yourself in each passing life with those who shine with your tones and vibrations to reach out as a collective ONE to those who need or are looking for greater meaning and wisdom to return home with.

See all those around you as the joyous friends and vibrational matches that you loved when you were not in the physical. Thankfully welcome them for the roles they agreed to share with you for the harmonizing of their souls to yours and the collective *oneness* of creation. Those you regard as someone who brings conflict into your life are also holy beings and soul connections, evolved such as yourself but forgetting the origins of their home as well. Although you may have an understanding of the significance of the people in your life, it is likely that you, too, permit yourself to be in conflict. This is a result of the amnesia of life. This has to be, so that your work, growth, and learning can be done in this brief instant of time called *life*.

I have come to realize that we are all here looking for the greater meaning of our lives. Many people ask themselves, *What is my purpose?* Feeling that you have no purpose is one of the greatest despairs of humanity. If you don't feel a reason to get up and start your day in the morning, it's difficult to want to carry on.

In my experience of seeking my greater purpose, I've sought understanding through the writings and teachings of others as well as my own innate wisdom. My seeking has been done primarily through exposure to the subjects of reincarnation, karma, past-life regression, Buddhism, stoicism, astrology, and other metaphysical subjects. My search has culminated in a new awareness and knowing—not knowing intellectually, but spiritually, innately, what we are all doing here.

Having processed all these experiences, it is as though I now understand the purpose of my life as Laura. I had the information before; the problem is that it was primarily being processed by my brain, not my heart. When you try to live under the illusion that you are in control of everything happening in your life, you potentially miss out on some spontaneous experiences. Inclinations to control everything are due to fear: fear of everything, fear of nothing, and fear of nothingness. Once you know that your happiness is your responsibility, you bring into your life only circumstances and people that help you achieve that. Any others will begin to fall away.

This is one of the real challenges of a spiritual awakening: when those you've known for years no longer vibrate at the same level as you. Cherished friends and loves drift away, and you find that your work is no longer rewarding or uplifting, potentially leading to decisions to change some components of your work. Don't be afraid to release what is no longer serving you for your highest good. What we generate inward is what we reflect outward among those we come in contact with.

Soul mates have been written about, sought after, longed for, and envied for ages. Many people still believe we get only one soul mate, who is our lifelong partner or spouse. That actually isn't true. We get the gift of many soul mates when we come into our life. There are the very close and intimate soul mates; for me, these are my spiritual partner and his sons. Close friends and family members are soul mates, and even some social or work colleagues are soul mates. Many groups of individuals, extending out like rings and representing all our many encounters, are also soul mates and soul groups.

Coworkers and schoolmates can also be great places for us to encounter old soul friends on our life path. They provide years of developing bonds that may last throughout our earthly lives and beyond. Each job or new class that you take can bring in new friends or foes; only in that particular time and space do we have the opportunity to meet them. Two of my coworkers and I all lived on the same block back about thirty years ago. Two of us lived there at the same time—Margie and me—and another counselor at a different time. It was funny to find out that Margie remembered seeing me in the neighborhood when I was a teenager.

Coworkers often become like second families or the family some didn't have. Our little work family is a reunion of souls coming together for the healing of others and ourselves. We get the chance to work out our own karmic balance with employers, coworkers, and schoolmates.

We're generally attracted to people based on a feeling they bring about for us at our initial meeting. When we are younger, we may judge people based exclusively on the external image we see. As that becomes a deeply engrained practice, the circle of friends we interact with reflects that initial judgment. There's an old saying I heard that goes something like this: "Show me your friends, and I will tell you who you are." If someone doesn't fit that profile, they are unlikely to get a chance to connect with you.

However, as we mature, our circle of friends changes to include more diverse individuals so that we may grow and also to reflect our maturing personalities. When I was younger, I had a very small network of friends that I hung around with. Now, thankfully, I've broadened my horizons. I have friends of different ethnicities and faiths and ages. A relatively new but good friend of mine is a Buddhist monk from Sri Lanka, Bhante Ethkandawaka Saddhajeewa. Ironically, we share the same birthday. He and another monk, Bhante Kottawe Nanda, also from Sri Lanka, opened a meditation center on Long Island about six years ago.

They came from Sri Lanka to New York to teach the Dhamma and meditation to us westerners. As a result I've been able to make more soul-mate connections than I ever would have imagined fifteen years ago. Like me, Bhante Saddhajeewa has had aspirations to be a social worker, and he successfully achieved this attending the same university I did. During that time, we became good friends as we discussed the wonderful profession of social work and the academic process he was undertaking. He hopes to bring social work to his home country, which doesn't have that profession. I look forward to supporting him in achieving that dream. We both agree that we were connected in a past life, likely as monks.

I can clearly see interconnected experiences in almost everything. I know we are all connected to each other, if even by a thread. When I hear something from anyone, such as new neighbor moving in or a client's emotional frustration about their families, I understand that it's purposeful to the bigger picture, which isn't all about *me*. It is all about *we*! As I've already mentioned, I do not believe any encounter is random.

Each and every one of us has a purpose. Not one of us ever comes into this world as insignificant on any level. We each have many life destinations that our soul is hoping to experience and grow from. We fulfill these goals throughout many lifetimes and with many life lessons learned.

Some individuals don't realize what the lessons were for until they graduate from this school of life. They often struggle with feelings of anger, uncertainty, and discontentment. There are some who reach a spiritual pinnacle in their lifetime, discovering their purpose and living from that space of knowing they are on the right path. Those are the people you encounter who have a joyful attitude and outlook about life, no matter what challenges they face. They generally emit an energy that makes you want to be around them.

As you go along this spiritual path and journey of life with a new awareness, you will suddenly notice more people coming into your life on the same path. You may find yourself saying "I just read about that" or "Someone at work was just telling me the same story" much more frequently. Look for the synchronicities. They are right there, waiting for you to notice them.

# Epilogue

There are many different parts and pieces of the spiritual puzzle of life and the afterlife. All are significant and lead to the same place. If I could identify a few of the most useful spiritual ideals in my life, the first would be that I can manifest anything with the recipe of a thought plus a splash of enthusiasm and a healthy amount of determination and discipline. I know that these ingredients equal the ideal outcome.

To contemplate is to consider something. It is the "hmmm, that seems like an interesting experience to have." Reflection is the process of determining if something is really what you want and how it will serve others. Enthusiasm is the fuel that sends the idea into the universal mind for preparation. Think of it as a rocket taking off from a launch pad and heading into space. Determination is your role in the partnership. For example, you're looking at office space for your new business venture or checking the prices of a sewing machine to start making clothes. All of these steps show Source or Spirit or the divine Creator that you are willing to do your part. Then watch the magic unfold.

The same recipe applies to things we don't want, like health problems. If we take the same ingredients of a thought, like "hmmm, I notice I have a mole on my arm," plus a pinch of "oh no, I think a lot of these kinds of moles are cancerous" (enthusiasm), and we add some investigation on Google, searching for information about cancerous moles, and talking to our friends about skin cancer (determination), we are launching rockets filled with fear of illness into the universe.

Then you go to the doctor to get the mole removed, and if it isn't cancer, you live in fear that if you get another mole, that one will be cancer. I use cancer only as an example, because it seems to be the disease that most evokes fear and hopelessness in the hearts and minds of millions of people.

This isn't a suggestion that you do nothing when you aren't feeling well. It's just a suggestion to change your thoughts and projections about illness to wellness. I've been saying for years, "I never get sick," and it's true; I really never get sick. I don't have fears and projections about it, and I don't dread or expect its arrival. Despite that, the New York State Department of Health requires that I get a flu vaccine; all hospital workers must get them or wear a surgical mask. There was a time I was able to decline the vaccine citing spiritual beliefs. That ended a few years ago. I'd never had the flu without the vaccine, but I didn't like the option of wearing a surgical mask eight hours a day, which would make my clients think I was sick. It concerned me that the suggestion of illness in a non-hospital setting would have negatively impacted the therapeutic process.

I've seen what the power of suggestion can do, depending on who it's coming from. If a doctor says to a patient, "You'll have a lot of pain after this procedure, so you'll need pain medication," the power of that suggestion is placed into the patient's psyche and then played out by the mind and body. This often results in a need for more treatment and more medication. This applies also to what individuals believe they are capable of achieving based on their family history or circumstances. If a child is told that no one in his family went to college or became a nurse or teacher or doctor, the suggestion is that the child shouldn't go in that direction. It may take a long time for that suggestion, however subtle, to be overridden.

Another significant spiritual awareness for me is that the afterlife is much more blissful and glorious than anything we can experience in the physical form. So many people fear it and function from a fear of death. I believe death is the best-kept secret. Just knowing that there's nothing you can do to get things wrong is quite liberating. That doesn't mean we have a green light to live recklessly. In fact, it's just the opposite. Knowing that for every action there is a reaction, even if it isn't in this lifetime, helps me to want to be the best Laura I can be. I don't want to cross over with remorse, with sadness over wrongs I'd committed against someone else, or with regret that I treated someone poorly or that I didn't attempt to do anything nice for someone. I want my life review with my guides to be wonderful. I want to know that when I go home, I'm bringing back more beneficial experiences then regretful ones.

I know that everything I do is recorded in my book of life, and this is true for everyone. The Akashic records (the term Edgar Cayce used to describe the book of life) consists of every thought and action we've had. Cayce stated the following regarding the Akashic records: "Upon time and space is written the thoughts, the deeds, the activities of an entity—as in relationship to its environs, its hereditary influence; as directed—or judgment drawn by or according to what the entity's ideal is." We will review everything we do between incarnations to determine where we excelled and where we faltered.

I believe that all religions, spiritual traditions, and metaphysical teachings blend perfectly like interlocking pieces of a puzzle to form a beautiful bigger picture. To create that picture, each piece is needed. Each religion has its own version of mysticism or something as simple as the golden rule that links it to another religion. The Kabbalah is the mysticism of the Jewish religion while the Gnostics were the mystics of the Christian religions. Islam has its mysticism in the traditions of the Sufis. Catholics have centering prayer, and Buddhists have mantra meditation. The Stoics had teachings similar to Buddhism. There are many Eastern spiritual traditions in addition to the well-known Confucianism, Taoism, Buddhism, and Hinduism. Ancient classical philosophers, such as Plato, paved the way for the arcane teachings of new-age thinkers, as they were called in the early 1900s. Ultimately, all the paths lead to the same place.

Then there is astrology, an important piece of the puzzle. *The sky is the time clock of the soul.* Early philosophers sprinkled within their great works the art of astrology, and most cultures of the world embraced it. It's defined as a science and a new-age metaphysical practice regarding the alignment of the planets and the houses, with just the exact degrees between each, that mark the perfect time for each soul to make another appearance into the physical incarnation. Within this time clock of the soul, we move through the conditions and circumstances of our life.

The strengths of our personality and the challenges we may face can be predicted and interpreted by an adept astrologer. If you have your exact birth information, I recommend you have your chart and transits done—an additional piece of the spiritual puzzle that can bring you deeper insights about yourself and your circumstances. I have an awesome astrologer, Joan Kilgen (vestaastrology.com). She has done my natal chart and transits for several years now, the readings are remarkable and extremely accurate. If you want to explore this part of your spiritual puzzle, you won't be disappointed.

Close to my heart and my daily life is Buddhism. I'm still a novice in the deeper teachings, but I consciously follow the Five Precepts and the Eightfold Path every day. *The Dhammapada*, a collection of verses of the Buddha, is a great way to begin to learn a little bit about Buddhist thought. The Buddha, Siddhartha, was born a prince in a wealthy family over 2,600 years ago. He was going about living his life, unsatisfied with what riches brought him spiritually. He started to question the meaning of his life and then started questioning the reality of life in general. The need to learn the answers to these questions led him to walk away from life as he knew it and venture out into the world and into nature to seek the answers.

His experiences brought him to places and meetings with people he would never have had the chance to encounter living behind palace walls. His awakening came through interacting with many types of people. He also observed the patterns of all living beings on the earth. He noticed how and why people suffer and why some others do not suffer. He wondered about the way people coped with living and dying and the reality of life, death, and birth. He spoke of the impact of thoughts on how people perceive their lives. He understood the law of attraction way back in the fifth or fourth century BC, recognizing that existence is an illusion. One of the verses in *The Dhammapada* says, "Master your words, master your thoughts, and never allow your body to do harm." He also spoke of sorrow: "Everything arises and passes away. When you see this, you are above sorrow. This is the shining way."

As it was for the Buddha, planted within each of us are signals to awaken and begin a more conscious walk along our spiritual path. The only thing that keeps us from recognizing these signals is our minds. Most of us live in a state of constant busyness and doing. It's difficult for us to allow ourselves to have quiet moments. Worse yet, we are afraid of the quiet moments and avoid them for fear of where our minds may travel. If you miss the signal to awaken, it returns again and again, giving you many opportunities—endless, in fact—to start investigating what the signaling feelings are.

The seeds have been planted for all of us to bloom in glorious and radiant ways. Self-limiting thoughts are what keep us from reaching our fullest potentials. Everything can be achieved when you start to see the magnitude of your creative abilities. Stop yourself from indulging in thoughts such as "I can't do that or "that is unlikely to happen" or "the odds are against me." Instead turn them around to something like "everything is within my reach" or I absolutely will achieve that goal."

There are times you may feel like you aren't getting anywhere or things aren't happening fast enough. When you feel discouraged, think of Aesop's fable of the tortoise and the hare, the tortoise gets to the finish line one little step at a time. So can you. Even though you may not be able to see the progress, have faith that the universal Creator is working behind the scenes to bring your heart's true desire. Even if you are not seeing immediate results in your life circumstance just having a positive outlook brings a happier state of mind, and that alone is an improvement. There may be times in which you encounter someone or something that really inspires you.

That may be just enough awareness for you to tap in to the truest inspiration, which is from your soul, your higher self. That timeless and eternal essence of *you* is where an endless sea of inspiration awaits. Reach out for it, and the gift of inspiration you seek will flow right to you like a beautiful waterfall cascading from a mountaintop.

# Acknowledgments

Thanks and appreciation to my mother, Joann, for your continued encouragement and feedback on my manuscript as it progressed and your overall enthusiasm about me writing this book

Thank you to my spiritual partner, William, for your willingness to give me the time and space I needed to complete my manuscript. Your notes and messages of encouragement and enthusiasm have been precious to me throughout the writing process.

I am grateful for my dear friend Ven. Ethkandawaka Saddhajeewa for his encouragement and confidence in my writing and the insights and messages I wanted to share on these pages. I am thankful to both Bhante Saddhajeewa and Ven. Kottawe Nanda for coming to Long Island all the way from Sri Lanka to teach the Dhamma.

I must mention someone I have never met, but whose gift of being an intuitive astrologer has guided me from afar. Joan Kilgen (vestaastrology.com) has been doing my transits for several years now, and her ability to interpret what was happening in my chart with what I was experiencing in my life during any given month has been so beyond accurate that it's sometimes uncanny. Thank you, Joan.

And finally, to all the individuals I've encountered who have sought healing on some level, my deepest thanks to each of you for sharing your experiences, strength, and hope with me throughout my twenty years as a therapist. May your journeys be filled with joy and inner peace.

Namaste.

Printed in the United States
By Bookmasters